# The Nine Rooms
## *of*
# Your Life

*Finding Happiness and Fulfillment
from the Inside Out*

## Valerie Althoff

FLOATING LEAF PRESS

Written by Valerie Althoff
www.avisioninplace.com

Illustrations by Ambrea Wright
www: ambreawright.com

Published in the United States of America by

FLOATING LEAF PRESS

A division of
WordPlay
Maureen Ryan Griffin
6420 A-1 Rea Road, Suite 218, Charlotte, NC 28277
Email: info@wordplaynow.com
www.wordplaynow.com

Library of Congress Control Number:2019918021
ISBN 978-1-950499-06-9

## Dedication

This book is dedicated most especially to the divine spark of Godness within, a loving and wise presence which has been an ongoing guide and catalyst throughout my life.

I'm also very thankful for the inspiration and guidance of all my teachers great and small, those who have touched my life and been an influence, knowingly or unknowingly, in the direction of my journey. They include my family, friends and people I've met along the way (you know who you are). I am humbled and grateful, and I thank you all.

# Contents

# Introduction

This book is in your hands because I finally mustered the courage to write it. For a long time, I really didn't see the point in adding yet another book to the world—there are a plethora of helpful books on how to live a good life on the market already, so why bother writing another one?

But clients and friends kept reminding me that not only is what I have to say important, but *how* I say it, through my words and perspective, is unique, and will therefore appeal to each reader in a way that other books might not. Every day my book isn't available, they said, is a day someone goes without the insights I may bring to them. I finally listened.

The postponement of writing *The Nine Rooms of Your Life* has given me the wonderful opportunity to experience what I've learned in new ways. This book is more than just theory, it's a compilation of what I've truly come to know is a powerful way for humans to live a full and balanced life. We are each a work in progress. Every day on the planet is a new opportunity to learn more about life and grow into more of who we are.

As we move through the experiences of our lives, we play various roles at different times—child, student, seeker, employee/employer, teacher, lover, partner, parent, friend, and a myriad of others. We all play different roles throughout our life, depending on our age, geographical location, and our individual connections with others. Each role we play, and each experience we have within that role, gives us the opportunity to grow in self-awareness. *Experience really is the best teacher.*

I like the analogy of theater and acting, because it's such a fun way to look at our life here on Earth. We come into the world as a child, playing the role of a child. As we grow, we take on the role of teenager, followed by the role of adult. Then, we play an assortment of roles, depending on our circumstances, desires, and goals. Some roles are played for life, such as a parent. Others, like being an employee, may change, offering different responsibilities and challenges as our situations change.

I believe we come into life as a human being with a *script* that we've written before we get here. This script is known deep within us, and we know it when we're born. (Have you ever seen babies who just look wise?) At some point in our first few years, most of us forget our script on a conscious level. But it's something we innately know—and it's with us throughout our whole life. And, like any script in a play, there is an overall theme, various adventures with different roles, and, finally, an ending, all of which are known before the play has even begun.

So it is with our life. We come in with a script and bring it to life by acting out our various roles with fellow actors until, at some point, we drop the body and the play comes to an end. Then, we can choose to come back with a different script next time, to play different roles.

In our life, these roles are called *experiences*. We may repeat aspects of the same script over and over, to practice challenging roles/experiences until we discover the meaning and value of them for ourselves.

In this book I share some of the wisdom I've gained as a result of experiences I've had playing various roles. My desire is that, in sharing my perspective, others may benefit in some way from it. I do not wish to say that my way is the right way, or impose my beliefs on anyone, only to share them with the hope that they will provide insights that will add value to your life.

I believe that all of us are where we are because it's where we need to be in the cycle of our life, as we work on our own script—and where we are is perfect for us. Therefore, if you read something here that resonates with you, great. If it doesn't, pass it by because it's not meant for you at this time.

*The Nine Rooms of Your Life* also reflects my spiritual journey. I've been seeking answers to the question "who am I?" all my life and I've finally come to know personally that I am—and, I believe, we all are—much, much greater than what the world, and even most religions, teaches. The most important journey of all is the one we live inside, and that's unique to each one of us.

One thing that's important to know about me is that I've been a feng shui consultant since 2001. Learning feng shui was a turning point in my life, a time when I began to see the world from the perspective of energy, and also see the value of understanding energy as the force that literally makes the world go 'round. As a consultant, I've connected with people from all walks of life, in their homes and businesses. The one thing everyone I work with has in common is they all desire to have, do, and be the best they can be in their lives—they all innately want to act out their script.

I believe making this happen begins with seeing life as energy in motion. The more we understand and are aware of this energy, the more we can sync it with our own desires and thus make them real in our lives.

As all life begins as energy, this book is written largely from my perspective of life as energy. From my commitment to a life devoted to a spiritual perspective, I've done research on energy as the life force that animates everything and everyone. Now I'm applying this knowledge to seeing how the flow or blockage of this energy affects various parts and pieces of a person's life.

Energy continuously cycles within and through the world and all life, from birth to death, at all levels of existence, from a single blade of grass to the universe and beyond. Energy never ends or dies, it simply transforms. At death, the body stops functioning when the soul (that spark of Godness that is us) decides to leave. But in truth, the organic material that makes up the body simply transforms into its base organic material . . . dust to dust. The energetic essence of who we really are continues on.

The earth is a closed system—that is, the air we breathe today is the very same air the ancient Egyptians breathed. It just keeps cycling around the planet. Trees take in carbon dioxide and give off oxygen, the purified air we need to live. This is why nature is so important. It's all an amazing, beautifully balanced and very complex creation of energy moving into and out of form. Humans thrive when they are able to attain and sustain that balance.

How you manage your own energy determines, and is determined by, your life experiences. To discuss the different arenas of life in which these experiences take place, I use the analogy of rooms in the house of your life. As you begin your own journey through this book, you'll feel the different energy of each aspect or room as it relates to your own life. You'll also come to understand the importance of living in every room or, in other words, living a wholistic life.

## Why Rooms?

I read a parable about a man who lived in a large house that had many rooms, but he chose to occupy only one room. In all the years he lived in this house, he was afraid to open the doors to any other room for fear of what might lie within. To make a long story short, there was a lesson at the end of his life, relating to all the missed opportunities and experiences behind those other doors.

While the man in the story was an extreme case, I believe that we miss out on many life experiences if we keep any of our rooms closed off. We need to open the doors and live fully in all the rooms in our house—all the roles we play that make up the whole of what we call our life. Doing this—living wholistically—brings us fulfillment, a deeper sense of who we are and how we fit into the greater context of life here on Earth.

Living wholistically means being aware of who you are in the context of how well you are in sync with all the various aspects of your life. The awareness that your life is made up of many aspects, or what I'm calling rooms, brings you closer to living your life's purpose. You have greater control over designing the life you really want to live . . . your heart's desire. Ultimately, this helps you live a more balanced and peaceful life, because you're occupying all the rooms that make up the house of your life.

When you live in your home, you spend time in the kitchen, bedroom, and other rooms many times over the years. In much the same way, you also move through the rooms of your life over and over again throughout your lifetime. You pass through the same rooms again and again, but each time you enter a particular room, you'll be a little more knowledgeable because you've had experiences that bring new awareness. Every time you spiral around to a room again, you'll see it with a different perspective.

Each time you enter a room, *you're* different. You bring a different energy and will live in it differently because your experiences have changed your perspective. This is called *personal growth.*

## The Nine Rooms

Eckhart Tolle gives a great example of what makes up a room in his book *The Power of Now.* He explains that furniture may be in a room, but it is not the room itself. The walls, floor, and ceiling define the room, but these are not the room, either. The room itself is energy and cannot be defined, only described through the physical things that are part of it.

When I speak of a room in your life, I'm talking about the different roles we play and the particular experiences that we have that are related to that particular room. I call these nine rooms:

Center
Life Path
Self-Awareness
Family
Opportunity
Success
Relationship
Creativity
Wisdom

The names of these rooms refer to feng shui teachings, and I've come to see that taking each of them into consideration as we move through our days gives us a wholistic perspective. Each of the nine rooms is unique, but they're all inter- connected, they all have value, and it's important to occupy all of them throughout your life.

You express each room or area of your life differently and each one feels different from the others. A house is made up of different rooms that have specific purposes regardless of the *roles* you are playing. So it is that the whole of your life is made up of different aspects, no matter your age and circumstances. At any one moment you may be a mom/dad, wife/husband, brother/sister, aunt/uncle, artist/banker, employee/employer, etc. You express each of these roles in different ways as you move through your life. Put them all together and you have a whole, integrated life, or a *house* that is uniquely you.

In the latter part of the book, I'll use the rooms analogy from the perspective of feng shui and share some interesting client experiences I've had. Feng shui is a valuable tool to help you see that your physical spaces reflect what's going on in your life, and vice versa, the issues in your life show up in your spaces.

I hope you enjoy reading *The Nine Rooms of Your Life*. May it inspire you to view your life from a new perspective and spark a new or greater awareness of what it means to live a wholistic life.

# The Wholistic Life

*The best day of your life is the one on which you decide your life is your own. No apologies or excuses. No one to lean on, rely on or blame. The gift is yours—it is an amazing journey, and you alone are responsible for the quality of it. This is the day your life really begins.*

- Bob Moawad

The Merriam Webster dictionary defines the word *wholistic* as a philosophy *"characterized by comprehension of the parts of something as intimately interconnected and explicable only by reference to the whole."*

It also goes on to say that 'wholistic' is a natural evolution of 'holistic' and that the 'w' brings the meaning full circle. I personally like the word wholistic because it includes the word "whole," which describes my intention for writing this book— to help you to live a whole and complete life. A *whole* life can only be explained and lived by the inclusion and interconnection of various *parts*—or, to use my analogy— rooms. A house is made up of many different rooms . . . and a well-lived-in house makes it *home*; the home that is called your life.

Let's consider a different analogy for a moment—using a car, with its many important parts, as an example of a wholistic life. The tire can only do its job when it is attached to a wheel or hub. Without this wheel, the tire is just a round piece of rubber. The wheel that holds the tire is attached to the car. Neither the wheel nor the tire is of any use without the driveshaft of the car, and the whole car won't go anywhere without the engine, which needs gasoline to move. When any one of these parts breaks down, the whole car stops moving forward. Ultimately, the whole car is useless without the energy source called gasoline.

This is like a human life. A breakdown in any one area (room) affects the proper functioning of the whole life. And life is only possible with input from an outside source (like gas for a car). I like to call this energy source Godness. I choose to call it Godness, not only because I believe God is conscious, pure love energy, but also because the word *God* has become so misconstrued, misused, and basically disrespected over the years. Many people have other words for this: One, Source, Spirit, All That Is, Allah, Atman, I Am, Universe, and others, but all refer to the same source of Creation.

## Our Homing Device

When our spark of Godness comes into form, it is *birthed* as a physical human being, but we are much more than this outer form. Deep within we have a *homing device,* or inner knowing of who we really are, which I have spoken of earlier as our script. The physical body grows and, because the outer world is so fascinating, it draws our attention away from our true *inner world*, and we begin to forget who we really are. But our homing device is always within. It gets our attention in surprising ways, one of which is intuition, an inner knowing we can't explain, but *something just doesn't feel right*. The beauty of our homing device is that it's always connected to our Godness, so it always knows the best choice for every experience. The challenge so many of us have is that we have a tendency to choose what our minds tell us is best, and dismiss the *gut feeling* of our homing device.

## The Importance of Understanding Energy

To get the most from this book, it's very helpful to take on the perspective that we are sparks of life force energy spending time in a body that's also energy in the form of skin, bones, and other natural material. The *essence* of who we are is a focused particle of this energy, something I refer to as

Godness. I like to use the metaphor of a sparkler, the little firework that's so popular with kids on the Fourth of July. Each of us is an individual spark of life energy that flew away from the One Sparkler or Godness, arriving here to spend time temporarily in the world of form.

This spark of energy is the same in each and every living thing—every species of plant, animal, and human on the planet. It is the life force that moves around, through, and within everything on the planet, as well as all planets, solar systems, galaxies, and universes. Everything and everyone are made up of this life force we call energy. It is only here, within a body, that we see unique and individuated forms. Outside everything is different, but inside we're all alike, we're all sparks of energy from the same mysterious divine source.

Energy is the creative life force, the underlying substance or mesh that ties everything together and makes it work. Think of energy as air (air IS energy). You can't see it (usually) but you breathe it in and can feel it as it blows across your face— and you certainly can't live without it. Like air, energy is always present; the world and everything in and on it is made up of it.

Philosophers and scientists have spent centuries trying to define and prove the mystery of the energy of life. It is now known that at a deep level of every cell is an atom, a spinning bit of energy. More recently, cutting-edge scientists are researching quantum theory and entanglement, based on discovering the origins of this mysterious life force that makes up our world and beyond, something that just *is*.

For sure, we have nothing to do with the beating of our hearts . . . yet there's *something* that keeps it beating every second of every day for years on end. Likewise, our breathing happens with no conscious control on our part. This is energy, or what I call Godness, the source of which is beyond our current understanding. To quote Tesla, "If you want to find the secrets of the universe, think in terms of energy, frequency, and vibration."

When we look at something with our eyes—say, for instance, a red apple, there's a lot happening on the level of energy that we're unaware of. The eyes are receivers of the energy waves that form a unique pattern we call an apple. This energy pattern passes through our pupils, onto the retina, and then to the brain. The brain processes and interprets this wave pattern as a red apple, because the brain has seen these patterns before and has *learned* to call them a red apple.

If the brain receives energy patterns it doesn't recognize—an energy pattern it's never been given before—it will either ask for more information or tell you to avoid it. You'll either be curious to know more about it or you'll turn away, depending on what you've been taught about approaching things that are new and different.

Without the brain to interpret what the eyes receive, we would see only patterns of energy, no matter what we look at, including people. Human bodies are simply focused pockets and patterns of energy that our brains have learned to interpret as specific people. Yet from the perspective of energy, we are simply pure energy. We are all literally made up of the very same stuff, just individuated into millions of slightly different patterns or forms we call bodies that all look different, so we can play at being human on the planet!

You may know someone who can see the energy patterns of things, and that's a wonderful gift, because they see beyond the physical appearance, with its enhancements and decorations. They know the truth about someone, because it shows up in their energy pattern. Even though most people can't see energy, they can still *sense* energy with the gift of intuition. Everyone has this ability but many aren't aware of it consciously. We all use our own energy in unique ways throughout our lives. To be sure, life on this planet is a wonderful adventure, one we came to act out and not take so seriously—but that's a subject for another book!

## Life Beyond the Physical

As I said previously, life in this physical world is energy in movement, coalesced pockets and vibrating patterns of life force that we see and interpret as various physical forms and then, based on what we've learned, label or name them. Before children know what to call something, before their brains have learned the names and labels of the energy patterns they see, all they see is energy. Children are little sparks of life force energy directly downloaded into a tiny body. Because they truly are not familiar with this physical world, they need to be taught what those patterns or forms are. This is called learning, and what a child learns early on determines the perspective and trajectory of his or her life.

Bruce Lipton, a neuroscientist and author of *The Biology of Belief*, says that, as a child, our subconscious mind is much like a tape recorder. For the first few years of life, a child's subconscious mind (the part of mind below waking awareness) is recording everything he or she experiences, because it is in the learning or receiving mode. They lack the critical filters that tell them something is good or bad, right or wrong. As that child grows and learns to think, she or he forms beliefs, biases, labels, and judgments based on the input from that tape recorder, and then they spend the rest of their life acting out of those recorded messages. We have all been "that child"—this is why it's so very important to become self-aware.

## Our Personal Energy Field

We each have a personal energy field, sometimes called an aura or etheric field, that surrounds and precedes us everywhere we go. When you meet someone for the first time, you get an immediate sense about them because your energy fields connect. When you meet someone, he or she may look fine and say the right things, but you may get the impression that there's something about them that feels off and not understand why. What happened is, your energy fields connected in the nano-second you met and you got a sense of that person beyond their physical presence. Your intuition was giving you important information based on the energy it connected with.

Single people often talk about wanting to have *good chemistry* with someone they meet, and if the chemistry isn't right, they're not interested. This chemistry they speak of is the intuitive energetic connection—if it feels good, it's good chemistry!

We are limited by our five physical senses because the energy we receive from them must be interpreted by the brain first, and this takes a bit of time. Lucky for us we have a sixth sense—our intuitive inner knowing—that is way ahead of the other five. Before your eyes or ears receive and send an energy pattern to the brain and the brain responds by telling you what you're seeing or hearing, your sixth sense already knows what it *feels* like on the level of energy. If you've ever walked into a room where everything looked fine but you got a sense that *something* just wasn't right, this was your intuition. We have a phrase for this: "I just can't put my finger on it." You walked into that room and your own energy field kicked in and your intuition gave you immediate feedback.

## Energy Just IS

Energy is neutral. That is, it's neither good nor bad—it just IS. However, our thinking mind, the one that develops with the growth of our conscious mind, likes to label and judge everything that comes into our awareness. It's this bias that makes the world what it is today, full of people who have different ways of looking at the same events and labeling them good, bad, right or wrong. The reality is that everything is simply occurring . . . it really is just what it is.

Conflict begins when two or more people see the same thing through their own biases or beliefs and they feel the need to defend them. If those people could simply *agree to disagree*, to understand that each are entitled to their own version of an issue and respect that of the other, there would be a lot less division in the world!

Michael Singer, author of *The Untethered Soul*, says the mind is the cause of all the world's problems. The mind has a label or judgment about everything, even the weather. If it's raining, the mind says, I don't like this rain! The truth is, it *is* raining, it does this often and it won't stop just because we don't like it. We could live a more peaceful life if we stopped listening to our mind's opinions and thoughts about everything and simply worked at accepting things just as they are. This is one way to live more wholistically—to face what *is* without judgment, learn from it and then move on. Adding opinions or thoughts about a situation only makes it a lot harder to move through it.

The highest and best thing we can say about anything is simply that it's different or unique. As you read these statements, listen to what your own mind is saying to you:

> *One style of clothing is not better than another.*
> *One breed of dog is not better than another.*
> *One part of the world is not better than another.*

Did you hear the mind wanting to take exception to one or more of these? Is it possible that some people simply prefer or like one more than the other? Consider reading these statements and accepting them as true from the perspective of IS-ness. They are simply statements of the difference of what IS.

Our habit of judging is disrespectful to what something or someone *is*. Because every single one of us is here on our own unique journey with our own script and we've grown up and live in totally unique ways, each of us has our own perspective on life, and we are all entitled to our own views and perspectives. We're all just trying to live our lives in the best way we can, given where we are on our journey, and we all deserve respect for that.

## Energy Is Meant to Flow

Energy, the life force that animates form, is meant to flow or vibrate at different levels. If energy becomes stagnant, *what is* changes. A dammed-up creek is no longer a creek—it becomes a pond that can grow stagnant with algae and weeds.

The movement of water is a good analogy to show the different ways energy flows: At room temperature water is liquid and flows where it's directed. Put fire under water and it turns to steam—the energy vibrates very fast. Put water in the freezer and it turns to ice—the energy vibrates *very* slowly. It's the same water, but the energy flows or vibrates at different speeds depending on what conditions it is exposed to. Liquid, steam, or frozen . . . it's still just water. One condition is not better, not more or less important than the other; each is valuable in different circumstances.

This is true for all of life: everything and everyone is a uniquely vibrating packet of energy, expressing this energy in an endless variety of ways and forms. We humans express our own energy in unique ways, from high vibration (laughter, exercise, excitement) to low (sleep, meditation, depression). This vibration or movement of energy is unique to each experience and each one has value. We express our unique spark of Godness through the example of how we live. What kind of example do you want to be?

## We Live on Four Levels

We're born into a physical body that holds our spark of Godness. We experience a world that's made up of many diverse energy patterns or forms that we come to know as people and things. We therefore exist on the *physical* level.

Another part of us is our thinking mind. The brain is our built-in computer or hardware, and the mind is like the computer program or software, which gives us a perspective of life on the *mental* level.

We have the ability to express and feel emotions, so we experience life on the *emotional* level.

We can communicate with and receive guidance from our connection with Godness through an intermediary of sorts, which some call Higher Self or Soul. This is the part of us that has knowledge of both physical and spiritual perspectives and is considered to be *who we really are*. It influences us on a deep inner or *spiritual* level.

Therefore, we exist on four levels simultaneously—*physical*/body, *mental*/mind, *emotional*/feeling, and *spiritual*/connection. As you read about each room, or area, of your life, I'll explain how the flow of energy can get blocked in that particular area and how to keep it flowing on all these levels. I'll give examples of the difference it makes in your life when the energy is flowing—and suggest things to do to help keep it moving.

# The Rooms

*We ought to walk through the rooms of our lives, not looking for flaws, but looking for potential.*

- Ellen Goodman

# Center

*There is no greater power in Heaven or on Earth than pure, unconditional love. The nature of the God force, the unseen intelligence in all things which causes the material world and is the center of both the spiritual and physical plane, is best described as pure, unconditional love.*

- Wayne Dyer

*Nature is an infinite sphere of which the center is everywhere and the circumference nowhere.*

- Blaise Pascal

The Center room is our core, the deepest part of who we are. It is our connection to the source of life energy from which we move out into the world to experience life. It is the beginning. . . of a life, an idea, an inspiration. Everything begins with this spark inside at the center that is our essence, our Godness. Words cannot begin to describe this benevolent energy that is the source of all life, out of which we were created.

We spring out of this Oneness as a spark of life that slides into a physical body. It is said that we *choose* to leave our *home in Oneness* to take on a body and have a multitude of experiences in the physical realm. We, as a spark of Godness in form, are eager to play the game of being a human being. It's a game in which we purposely forget that it's a game, we forget who we really are, and after many experiences and (I believe) many lives, we begin to remember the truth of who we are and why we're here.

Before we're born and haven't yet forgotten who we are, we formulate a plan, an agenda or script of what we want to accomplish when we come into human form, which is designed to help us remember. This plan consists of what are sometimes called *life lessons*. I think they're called that because some of them take a whole life to learn!

The Center is an energy that originates from Godness. This *divine* energy radiates out to affect how we live in the other rooms. This core of who we are is like the foundation that strengthens and gives meaning to the other areas of our life. The health and balance of each *room* in the cycle is influenced by this core of who we are. Simply put, how you live your life is greatly influenced by the plan that comes from your heart, which is the connection to Oneness. This means that you are not only the compilation of all aspects of your life, but your life experiences are enhanced (or disrupted) by how well you're aware of and connected to this core. If you lose the balance that is necessary for the optimal functioning of your center, it affects all areas of your life.

This Center room of your life is the *source* which encompasses the totality of who you are on the physical, mental, emotional and spiritual levels. This is literally the pivotal area around which your life revolves and it needs your care, love, and attention.

Body workers understand the importance of working on the core or center of the body. A strong core allows you to achieve ease of movement and balance. They know that a balanced body is a stronger body and it begins with the core or center. Just as a strong and balanced body is the foundation for a healthy physical life, a strong and balanced Center allows you to achieve a more balanced and harmonious inner life.

Blocking the flow of this energy will affect every area of your life in some way because the energy here radiates out from the center, like the sun's rays radiate out to everything, regardless of its nature. When you are physically, mentally, emotionally and spiritually centered, you'll be better prepared to face the challenges that come up in any room on the cycle of your life.

# Gratitude

I mentioned the heart beating and lungs breathing. Do you realize what a gift this is, what a miracle? Our heart beats and breathing simply happen, every second of every day we're here. Being grateful for this amazing gift is a way of connecting to source, because it's a recognition that you are aware of something greater than your small self. Speak a humble *thank you* to whomever/whatever you believe created you—and do it often—the energy will be returned, and this simple act keeps the connection flowing!

# The Value of Living in This Room

The Center represents the foundation of your life, and it's important that you thrive here. It is in this centered place that you receive more energy from Godness to continuously replenish the energy you expend in the cycle of your life. You can only do this by maintaining some kind of connection. What this looks or feels like for you is completely up to you. In truth, it doesn't matter how you keep the connection open, only that you do. Just as a lamp needs to be plugged into an outlet to receive its source of energy (èlectricity) to light the bulb, we need to "plug in" and connect with the source of our energy, so we can be a *light* in our world.

There are levels of this connection that happen without our awareness. The heart beats, the lungs fill with air, and digestion takes place, all without our thinking about it. But our awareness of and appreciation for the beauty of this amazing connection—one we experience throughout our whole life—boosts the energy we receive to better assist us in other areas of our life.

## If the Energy of This Room Is Not Flowing

Physical

Your energy resources become weakened, including your immune system, and you become vulnerable to sickness and disease. You have no energy to go out and experience life. You may forget that the body is a physical form that was created in love, with love, by a love beyond understanding.

Mental

Your brain doesn't receive all the energy it needs and you lose clarity and sharpness. You may become confused about what to do and how to manage your life and have trouble staying focused.

Emotional

You may experience a number of emotional imbalances: apathy, depression, confusion, frustration, and a sense of disconnectedness from people, nature, and the world in general. You may not have a desire for living.

Spiritual

You begin to feel like you're alone in the world. You can lose your sense of purpose and meaning because it's in your Center where you connect to and come to know this. You may find yourself thinking, "Nothing matters, I don't feel like I belong here."

## When the Energy of This Room Is Flowing

You have a deep sense of well-being or knowing in your core or center, because it comes into and flows through you as a result of your connection to it. In order to be *a light in the world* it is imperative to maintain this connection . . . to stay plugged in! This gives you a sense of a foundation from which you can move out into the areas of your life.

You understand that your body is the only one you get, so you take care of it as your only vehicle.

## How to Keep the Energy of This Room Flowing

Physical

➢ Maintain the body's health and strength by eating well.
➢ Give your body regular exercise (something that you enjoy doing!)
➢ Get sufficient sleep and the rest your body needs to perform at its best.

## Mental

➢ Practice meditation or time in solitude (whatever way works for *you* is best) as a way of connecting to and receiving inspiration from your center.

➢ Read inspirational books.

➢ Join like-minded groups to help you stay connected.

➢ Keep a journal, or simply write down thoughts that inspire you.

## Emotional

➢ Be willing to accept and embrace even difficult experiences by getting in touch with how you feel and learn from that.

➢ Don't resist the tough emotions. Allow yourself to feel them instead of stuffing them. This frees you up to see the situation more clearly and helps you move through it because you're not stuck in the emotional upheaval of whatever it is.

➢ Let go of emotions that no longer serve you. Sometimes people actually become comfortable with a feeling of anger or sadness, not realizing that it affects how they live their life. They've managed to shove it out of conscious awareness (who, me? I'm not angry, you say angrily) but it still festers inside because they fear the feeling of it. Welcoming and deeply feeling something uncomfortable is important because it's the only way to clear it out. And when you've moved through the feeling of it, don't hang on to it!

> Remember that there is a purpose for every experience.

## Spiritual

> Develop a deep sense of value and purpose. This gives you a solid foundation from which to move out into all areas of your life.

> Attend a church or spiritual center that feels good.

> Ponder on inspiring poetry written by Rumi, Mary Oliver, and others who share vision, light, and love in their writings.

> Pray (or engage in whatever method you use to connect) for deeper insight and inspiration.

# Life Path

*We all have our paths in life we are supposed to follow to find who we are supposed to be, but it's not always a straight path. There is something inside of us that guides us, and if you are quiet and listen to it, you'll be all right.*

- Kyan Douglas

*Life would have been easier for me if I had taken the ' path of least resistance.*

- Michael Gove

When we live according to our plan or life lessons, we feel good and our choices feel good. When we feel good, it means we're on track. When we feel *off* in some way, it's a sign that we're headed in the wrong direction, as an inner message to shift back into that feel-good place by getting back on track. This is our inner homing device I mentioned previously.

So many people haven't learned to recognize this signal or inner voice I call intuition. This is why, for example, some who have shut off this inner voice so profoundly that they end up in jail. I taught life skills classes to inmates in a county jail for a while, and I used the homing signal analogy with them. I showed them how they'd gotten so far off track in their life that they couldn't sense this signal anymore, so it took d*ivine intervention*—angels in the form of officers in uniforms and badges—to put them in a *time-out* called jail so they could learn how to get back on a good track again.

Each one of us knows if we're open to that connection, to sense the signal that helps us stay on the track to live our life purpose. No one can do it for us, it's truly an inside job. Books will teach us how to do it, but we must take that final step into discovering it ourselves. We made the initial step by coming into a body to this physical realm, and we live a good life by maintaining that inner connection . . . our homing signal.

When we take on a physical body, we have experiences based on the plan we came in with. It's what I call living on purpose. Being able to do this smoothly and easily comes from paying attention to our *intuition*.

Intuition is also called a gut feeling or inner knowing. It's a wonderful gift and tool to help us know if we're heading in a direction toward or away from our purpose. We all have intuition, but many ignore it in favor of the mind. Then we *think* we know; something *makes sense* or is logical. But because we are beings made of energy, our intuitive or energy sense is our best form of guidance. We've all done something that didn't feel right—our heart connection or intuition said not a good idea. But because we *thought it made sense,* we went ahead with it anyway—and suffered through the experience.

We have a saying based on this truth: "my heart isn't into it." This means that our intuitive knowing is trying to tell us to make a different choice. Intuition is most often a very subtle sense, or what some call that "still small voice within." Our outer world, and the mind, can be very seductive and loud, but our inner knowing comes to us through our center, or heart, so it's wise to pay attention to how something *feels.*

## Life Plans and Life Lessons Are Unique

Because each one of us comes in with a unique agenda or life plan, we each have a unique perspective on life, and we are each living out experiences according to this inner plan. It therefore makes no sense to judge anyone else. We just *do not know* what anyone else is working on in their Life Path journey.

We've all heard of couples who come home from a vacation with very different opinions about it: one says it was wonderful and the other says it was boring. Same experience, different perspectives; each person living the experience in their own way. Neither is right or wrong, they simply have different perspectives of the same experience because of where they are on their own life path. So when several people come together, there will always be differing opinions about the same experience. You know how true this is if you've ever been to a family reunion!

We choose the events of our life to have experiences that are designed (consciously or unconsciously) to help us learn and ultimately remember who we are and why we came here in the first place. But as we all know, this physical world is very enticing, and we can get wrapped up in all the diversity (and detours!) it has to offer and forget about our life plan. This is why intuition is so important.

## The Power of Meditation

The outer world is chaotic, there's always something happening to distract us and keep our attention focused externally. Meditation is a powerful tool to help us connect to our center and learn more about our life lessons. It allows us to shut out the physical world and tune into the connection that's always there but is too quiet to hear over the persistent thoughts of the mind.

*How* you meditate is totally up to you. There are many books on the topic with advice from people who practice the way that works well for them—which may not fit you at all! There is no right or wrong way to meditate, but you do have to put yourself in a quiet space, away from any distractions: this means shut off your phone, put the animals in another room, and turn off the tv.

If you've never meditated before, be patient! Meditation is like any other exercise: there's a learning curve, it takes time to build the muscle, and it needs to be done regularly.

If you don't know how to start, just put yourself in a chair, close your eyes, get comfortable and let all thoughts just pass by. The idea is to forget about the body and the mind. Don't pay any attention to the mind when it runs on about this being a dumb idea (minds just don't want to be left out and will persist in thinking) and simply open yourself up to the possibility of hearing that still small voice within.

## The Value of Living in This Room

The room of the Life Path is the beginning of your journey in the world as a human being. It is the unique-to-you perspective from which you experience life. Not one other person on the planet will see the world the way you do. You may have similar experiences, but what each one takes away from that experience will be slightly different.

There is a reason why we're here. You may not know this on a conscious level, but each of us has a deep sense that our life here means something.  Many people find meaning in their life through living with a partner, having children, establishing a career. Relationships and experiences are the ways we *express* our purpose here. The love you have for your family or friends is an expression of the powerful energy of love that is the source of creation. The joy you feel when you do something you love to do is expressing the joy of creation. The deeper meaning of every experience is always rooted in how we express that love and joy.

This is why it's very important to visit this room often, to stay in touch with that sense of purpose and meaning.

## If the Energy of This Room Is Not Flowing

Because this room is about your life path, you lose your way and find it difficult to determine a clear direction in your life.

Physical
Because the body is your vehicle to get you around on the planet, it can also lose its sense of purpose. I think this is what fibromyalgia is—a general bodily malaise and pain based on energy blockage. The body is energy in form and its purpose is to serve us. When we lose our way, the body does as well. This manifests as fatigue, body aches, and lethargy.

Mental
Thoughts become scattered and diffuse, you "can't think

straight" anymore. Your mind reaches for all kinds of ways to help, and you can become overwhelmed by it all.

Emotional
You become apathetic about life, as in "what's the use?" and even depressed (our purpose is *pressed down*). You blame others, saying they "push my button!" because you forget that it's your button!

Spiritual
Because there is no longer a sense of purpose in being here, you can become very selfish. You lose sight of the bigger picture that all life is interconnected, and it becomes all about *me*. "Just Do It" becomes your motto, and you forget that what you do or think affects others.

## When the Energy of This Room Is Flowing

Life feels good. You get up every day with the sense that "everything is right in the world." The body is strong and healthy, and your thinking is sharp and clear. New ideas "just come to you" because you're connected to Godness, which is the source of inspiration.

# How to Keep the Energy of This Room Flowing

<u>Physical</u>

- ➤ Walking in nature helps to keep the body moving, plus it's good energy!
- ➤ Get plenty of rest to replenish the body. Just like you do maintenance on your car to keep it running, when you maintain your body, it serves you well!

<u>Mental</u>

- ➤ You may enjoy reading books about people who are living or have lived their purpose.
- ➤ Do a daily meditation or contemplation to sustain the connection to your center.

<u>Emotional</u>

- ➤ Give thanks that you're not alone in this world and be thankful for all your connections!
- ➤ Practice seeing your life as a gift, given from a source that knows you on a much deeper level than you do at this point!

<u>Spiritual</u>

- ➤ Follow your inspiration! Do things that fulfill you, pursue experiences that have meaning.
- ➤ Meditate and contemplate on different spiritual words.
- ➤ Start a gratitude journal as an ongoing reminder of all the good things happening in your life. (My publisher, Maureen Ryan Griffin, has written one called *The TAG,*

*I'M IT! Daily Practice: A Three-Month Journey of Thanksgiving, Acknowledgement, Gratitude, and Intention).*

# Self-Awareness

*Just keep coming home to yourself. You are the one you've been waiting for.*

- Byron Katie

*Knowledge of the self is the mother of all knowledge. So it is incumbent on me to know myself, to know it completely, to know its minutiae, its characteristics, its subtleties, and its very atoms.*

- Khalil Gibran

As the body grows, you also grow through learning about the world, who you are in relation to your world, how you fit into it, and what you want to do. This learning involves education, mostly in schools that teach you the basics of learning that are considered necessary for you to become *a productive member of society*.

Then you graduate from this necessary world-learning and become an individual *someone*—and because you got so wrapped up in learning about how to make your way in the world, you probably forgot who you really are and where you came from.

Some people are able retain awareness of who they really are through these years of learning. These are the ones we say are gifted, those who can see beyond the physical and use their intuitive sense. They are no different from us, it's just that they're consciously tuned into and trust their inner guidance.

Unfortunately, schools typically do not teach about life, nor do they really prepare us for life as an adult. We learn basic information that will prepare us academically but not socially, so when we *graduate* from that system, we are turned out into a world that's far more complex and diverse than anything we ever learned in school!

What we know about the world before adulthood is mostly what we're taught to know about it. As we enter adulthood, we learn about the world in an experiential way, and discover that it's a lot more complex and confounding than we could ever have imagined in school. If the world doesn't live up to our expectations based on what we learned, we get disappointed or disillusioned and then spend our lives trying to figure out why we're not really happy. This then becomes our challenge—to BE the best we can be, not just define ourselves by what we DO.

## Happiness from the Inside Out

Many humans live in the *pursuit* of happiness, thinking, I'd be happy if . . . This is because we keep looking outside; we think it's the world that can make us happy. In general, we aren't taught to remember the truth that happiness comes from inside, because those doing the teaching have also forgotten. If we're happy inside, we bring that energy into all of our experiences. If we don't feel this inside, we look to the world and others for our happiness. This makes for dysfunctional relationships, because we then point the finger at someone else for making us unhappy or not living up to our expectations of them to keep us happy. If we are innately happy, we don't need anyone or anything to make us happy and we can accept them as they are.

## Know Thyself

Self-awareness goes beyond learning. It's about knowing who you are inside, in your center, that connected piece of who you really are. This is the room for taking an inner inventory to know what's really important to you, what has meaning and value in your life. This takes courage and time. Facing the truth of who you are is not always pleasant, because we're human with human failings. Self-awareness is much more than forgiving yourself because you stole money from your dad's wallet when you were 15 and then lied about it.

Being self-aware means knowing what you believe, what principles you live by, what sustains you spiritually, and what is important to you.

Why do you behave the way you do? A person who is self-aware will know the answer to that question. If you continue behavior that doesn't feel good to you, It's likely that you are hanging onto a belief that needs to shift.

Have you really taken a good look at your beliefs? Can you write a list of them? Once you see your beliefs, the next step is to evaluate whether they still serve you.

Using myself as an example, I've believed for years that I'm a survivor, because I overcame many challenges in my early life. Recently I looked deeper at that belief and asked myself why I still believe that, because my life is not one of survival anymore. To my surprise, I discovered that I still believe I'm a survivor because I'm holding onto a deeper, more ingrained belief that life is hard! And that belief is based on unexamined experiences and beliefs in my life as well.

## What You Think About Is Likely to Come About

Energy is an *attractive* force; that is, you attract the energy that matches your thoughts. Basically, what you think most about is what you get. Energy doesn't understand words, it only heads toward the energy that matches it, or how you *feel* about what you're thinking that attracts it. If you think and say, "I don't want to get sick!" and you hold on to the fear that you could get sick, the matching energy of *sickness* is coming your way because you're hanging onto the thoughts and feelings about sickness. If you really want to avoid getting sick, keep your focus on how good it feels to be well. Or if you're sick, hold your focus on knowing how good you *will* feel to be healthy again—and <u>that</u> is the energy that you're attracting and will come your way.

It's true that we can have what we want, but we must be careful to watch our thoughts and focus only on what we <u>do</u> want. Saying affirmations is great, but your mind can sabotage them if it still holds onto thoughts of worry or doubt. If that's the case, you're putting out mixed signals, so you probably won't get what you want. It's really important to become more aware of *all* your thoughts. If you continue to struggle to have what you want in your life, dig deep inside to find any thoughts/beliefs/habits you may be holding onto that are blocking the matching energy of what you want.

As I mentioned earlier, energy is a vibration. When you hold onto thoughts of what you desire, your own energy is vibrating at the level of that desire. Because of the Law of

Attraction, what is coming to you is matching your own vibration. This is why hanging onto fear can only bring you what you fear. . .the matching vibration is that of fear.

You may have heard this story:

A Cherokee elder was teaching his grandchildren about life. He said to them, "A fight is going on inside me. It is a terrible fight between two wolves. One wolf is evil: he is fear, anger, envy, sorrow, regret, greed, arrogance, self-pity, guilt, resentment, inferiority, lies, false pride, competition, superiority and ego. The other is good: he is joy, peace, love, hope, sharing, serenity, humility, kindness, benevolence, friendship, empathy, generosity, truth, compassion and faith. This same fight is going on inside you and every other human being." The children thought about this for a bit, and then one asked, "Grandfather, which wolf will win?" He replied, "The one you feed the most."

## Beliefs Are Made, Not Born

We come into this life with a blank slate, a pure open mind. We form beliefs in early childhood that are either imposed on us by others (indoctrinated), or we form them based on either personal or vicarious experiences. Either way, it's very important to be aware of your beliefs and then decide if you want to keep them or let them go. As Plato said, "the unexamined life is not worth living." You are like a puppet pulled here and there by life if you don't know who you are. People who simply live life out of their unconscious beliefs often do not take responsibility for their actions. This can show up as a victim mentality.

## What Do You Value?

Just as knowing your beliefs is very important, it's also critical to know what you most value in your life. This gives you the freedom to make conscious choices and decisions for yourself—and when you interact with others. You have the right to be around people who share your values and avoid situations that don't align with them.

If your values aren't clear to you, you may end up in a relationship with someone who doesn't have the same values as you and then you wonder why you're not happy together. If you value owning a house and living there forever but your partner values moving to new locations frequently, for example, your values don't align. This could cause conflict. There is nothing wrong with having different values—as I said earlier, we're all unique. But if you don't talk about them before making a commitment to a long-term relationship, chances are pretty good it will be a challenge. If you must both continually compromise to make the relationship work, it probably won't.

Knowing what you believe and what you value—being self-aware—is the way to have more happiness and fulfillment in your life.

# Keep the Well Full

There is a difference between *selfish* and *self-first*. The world looks askance at people who put themselves first, but the truth is, it's very important to value yourself above anyone else– and it is **not** selfish, it's called loving and respecting yourself. The motto is, *self-first but no one else is second.*

There is a well inside us, a well of energy that we need to keep filled. We go through our days dipping into this well of energy and giving from it—to our family and friends, at work, through volunteering–and our well gets depleted. If we don't take care of ourselves first to replenish this well, it goes dry and we have no more energy for ourselves *or* for others. And then we wonder why we're tired all the time.

I think the profession of nursing gives us a great example of the need to keep our own well full. Nurses are notorious for giving and giving, a wonderful and admirable trait, but they give until their well is dry and then they get off balance themselves! I've seen so many great nurses suffer because they put everyone ahead of themselves. They give all their energy away, keep none for themselves, and then don't replenish their own well so they're prone to get depressed and even sick. Everyone, but especially anyone in the *giving* professions, must put themselves first and take care to keep their own energy well full to overflowing, so they can give without depleting themselves.

So many people work at jobs that drain their energy. They don't like what they do. They receive little or no recognition for the work they do. And when they get home, they're

drained so they have little energy to give
to their loved ones. They maybe have a drink or two, gulp
down some food, sit in front of the TV for a few hours
(another energy drain, by the way), fall into bed and sleep
poorly. Then they wake up the next day and do it all over
again—with even fewer energy reserves, because a few hours
of restless sleep are not enough to replenish that well! If they
ignore a depleted or empty well long enough, they get so off
balance that they will very likely get physically or mentally
sick.

Most of us are taught at a very early age that "it's better to
give than to receive" but if we don't continue to *receive*
energy to keep that well full, we simply cannot give without
hurting ourselves. Think of this as a continual cycle—you must
first *receive* energy so you can give it. When your well is full,
you happily give of yourself to someone. The other person
receives this gift of energy. Their energy of gratitude
replenishes your well so you can give again. It's a continual
cycle of give-receive-give-receive.

This is the perfect time to mention a term I learned a while
back: *energy vampires*. These are people who, after you've
been with them a while, leave you feeling tired or drained;
they literally *suck the life out of you*. They've benefitted by the
gift of your energy but didn't give you any in return. This is
because, on some level, they don't know themselves. They
need something from you and others that they believe they
lack. Because their well is not full and they don't know how to
replenish it, they look outside of themselves, either through

interactions with people or exciting and thrilling (and ultimately empty) experiences.

We all know people who are a joy to be around. These people exude lots of good energy and we love being around them. Their well is filled to overflowing and their energy is almost palpable. And because we enjoy being around them, we are at once *receiving* the overflow of their energy and *giving* back to them with our happiness in being around them—the give-receive cycle is working full blast and we all feel great!

The author Don Miguel Ruiz has written several books on how to deepen our sense of who we really are. His book *The Four Agreements* speaks about making powerful agreements with ourselves to stay in touch with our authentic or true self. In his book *The Voice of Knowledge* he writes that education teaches us *who we are not* and true self-awareness comes from inside. I highly recommend reading these books to gain understanding about the importance of knowing and maintaining your true sense of self.

From an energy perspective, the motto should be "receive before you can give." Find ways to replenish your well of energy by doing things you love to do, things that inspire you. Make it a habit to begin your day with a full well, because life often has a way of draining it quickly. This is why self-first is not selfish!

## The Value of Living in This Room

Self-awareness is beyond learning. First you learn about something, like education in school. Then, as a result of an experience, you come to know it. First you *learn about* it, like reading books about playing a piano. Then you have the *experience* of it, the feeling of actually putting your fingers on the keys of a piano, and finally (with practice) you can say you know how to play a piano!

Unlike learning, knowledge is a forever thing. You can read all the self-help books on the shelves today, you can talk to counselors for years, and you will *learn about* how to help yourself, but you must take that final step—to *experience* who you are yourself. A Chinese proverb says, "Teachers open the door, but you must enter by yourself." Those are valuable words for living in this room where you become self-aware.

## If the Energy of This Room Is Not Flowing

### Physical
You stop paying attention to the body. You may not keep it clean or feed it well, so you lose good hygiene habits. The body may have indigestion, weight issues, hair or teeth loss, and illness.

### Mental
You become forgetful and stop thinking about what matters, what's important to you. You may focus on taking care of

everyone except yourself, because you may believe others are more important.

You will not be aware of or will lose a deep sense of self. You may find yourself saying, "I just don't know who I am anymore!"

Emotional
You don't love or accept yourself, so you have nothing to give and can become depressed. It may become difficult to have meaningful relationships because you are unable to relate to anyone.

Spiritual
Because you lose your sense of a connected self, you see no reason to go within. This causes energy drain because you're not receiving. You feel alone and unworthy of being in the world.

## When the Energy of This Room Is Flowing

Because you're in touch with who you are on all levels, you have lots of energy and feel a sense of fulfillment at the end of the day. You are aware of your personal value to yourself and others and have self-love. Your own well is full so that you can freely and easily contribute to others. This is how you make a difference in the world!

## How to Keep the Energy of This Room Flowing

Physical

> ➢ Pamper yourself once in a while . . . get massages and pedicures.
> ➢ Include daily movement in your life. Walk, run, stretch dance, cycle, take yoga, spin, Zumba classes— whatever feels best to you.
> ➢ Treat yourself to enjoyable experiences—because you're worth it!

Mental

> ➢ Keep self-affirming thoughts in your head and don't listen to the critical mind.
> ➢ Every time you look at yourself in the mirror, say "I love you!"
> ➢ Read about people who overcame adversities, like Nelson Mandela and Maya Angelou.

Emotional

> ➢ Develop a sense of self-acceptance, which will bring more peace into your life.
> ➢ Do things you love to do, things that inspire and fulfill you.

Spiritual

> ➢ Read books by Wayne Dyer, Michael Singer, Don Miguel Ruiz and others who help you to see who you really are.

➢ Know *your Five Love Languages* (from the book by Gary Chapman) and share them with those who love you so they can help you fill your well. Don't forget to return the favor.

# Family

*I can't claim my grandfather's work has influenced mine directly, but his life certainly inspired me to follow this path.*

- Kevin MacDonald

*If the means were available, we could trace our ancestry back to the first blob of life-like material that came into being on the planet.*

- Clifford D. Simak

In this "family" room of your life, you learn who you are in relationship to your immediate relatives, which includes your parents, siblings, spouse or significant other, and children. This room also includes your family of origin and ancestry.

You come to know a larger picture of yourself in relationship to both your current family and those who came before you. This is called your *identity* or personality (your personal self) and is a compilation of the culture, traditions, beliefs, biases, patterns and habits that you share with family, as well as those that have been passed down to you.

When we first enter this room as a child, our minds are like blank slates. We come into this world totally open to receiving input. Very soon we learn traditions and beliefs that are indoctrinated or imposed on us. We're taught the ways of the family we live with and, because we lack the critical-thinking filters at this stage in our life, we soak all this up and take it in as truth.

Often, this is where prejudice (our tendency to pre-judge) begins. Without any filters to help us decide if we agree with what we are being taught or not, to decide whether it's right or wrong, we just go along with what is told—or shown to us. Our learning doesn't come from only what is said or taught verbally. We also take on the attitude of others and the example of how they live. Children may get the "do as I say, not as I do" message from their parents, yet most often it's what the parents do that has a bigger impact. It's true that actions speak louder than words. How often have you heard someone say (or said yourself), "I've become just like my mother/father!"

As was said earlier in this book, it's always a powerful thing to examine your beliefs. You may discover that you're hanging onto an old belief that's holding you back from where you want to be in your life now.

Some beliefs are below our level of conscious awareness—they're so deeply entrenched that we just continue to live them, even if they are keeping us from the life we really want to have. Questioning old beliefs and working to uncover hidden beliefs is a wise thing to do. It frees us up to live an authentic life.

## What Is Family?

Many people think of family in a nuclear sense, as in those people we live with, which typically includes our parents, children and others living in the same space together. But in times past, family embraced a wider circle of aunts, uncles, cousins, nieces, nephews and other relatives.

I think family also includes those who love and support us and even caretakers and co-workers who share similar interests and values. Then, there is the more challenging definition of family which includes all of us, as a *family of Man*, or the family of the human race. We seem to have a way to go before we can see everyone else on the planet as family members, but I do believe this is part of our journey into coming to know who we are.

## Ancestry and Beliefs

Throughout our childhood and many of our adult years, our relationships with the family in our lives are ones we consider most valuable.

Later in life, this room is important because it's a treasured part of who you've become. You begin to look at who you are through the context of ancestry, and how the wisdom of your ancestors influences how you experience life. Here you decide to either continue the traditions and culture of your family, or simply find ways to honor them.

We are the embodiment of all the wisdom passed down from our elders. One day you will be—or have perhaps already become—one of those elders as you share the wisdom you've gained through all your life experiences with your younger family members.

Plato wrote, "the unexamined life is not worth living." Again, there's a lot of truth to this, when you consider that much of who you are is the result of all the energy of family traditions and beliefs that have come before you. You may look like your grandmother or have the same mannerisms as your grandfather. You may have learned to speak Italian because it's the language of your ancestors. Your home may be filled with furniture, paintings, or relics that were passed down from one generation to the next—all treasures from your ancestors. It's this aspect of your life, in this room, where you take a serious look at how much of this history is true for you and how much of this is who you are. Your parents and family may want you to go to school to be a doctor, to be another in a long line of doctors before you. Or you may be urged to go into priesthood because generations before you did so. You may feel pressure to do so, even though your heart is calling you to go in a different direction.

A belief that's passed down through tradition and lineage is a powerful energy that has been built up over generations. If you try to break away from this energy, you may be hit with a lot of resistance. It's up to you to decide what is important to you, because you're the one who lives your life. A fulfilling and happy life depends on you being authentically you, not someone who has lost your sense of self trying to make your life fit into what others believe is best for you.

Every generation has beliefs that were formed based on the ways of the world of their time. Each new generation breaks away from the previous one because the energy of their world is different, and that new generation wants to do something new and different to *help make the world a better place.* The Baby Boomers are famous for how loudly and creatively they broke away from the traditions and ways of their older generation.

## The Value of Living in This Room

If there were one word for the value of this room, it would be *connection*. Here, you are connected with the family you live with, your wider circle of relatives, and the people you think of as family because of the love you feel for each other. As you grow in wisdom, you begin to understand that who you are is the result of your connection to the family that came before you, where you get a sense of the *wholeness* that your life is much greater than just you and your life here now. You are part of a lineage that has kept the energy of your particular family connection strong for generations before you. You appreciate that who you are today is the result of the synchronicity of the many connections that happened before you. You're here as you are today because your mom connected with your dad. They are or were here because their moms and dads connected with others who became your grandparents . . . .and so on down the line of ancestry. The dots are connected a long way back, and they all connect forward—to you!

## If the Energy of This Room Is Not Flowing

Stuck energy in this area of your life keeps you from moving forward in a wholistic way to embrace what's ahead. Because you don't have a deeper sense of who you are, you won't have all the resources you need to move ahead into achieving your true heart's desire.

Physical

Your body is the form that holds the spark of life energy that includes the energy of all those who came before you. The body carries this lineage in cells called *genes*. If the body is not honored as such, its systems and functions can slow down, causing health imbalances.

Emotional

You begin to feel confused about who you are and lose a sense of purpose. Traditions have little meaning and you lose the joy of holiday celebrations. Family gatherings become a chore and a challenge, something to suffer through. You feel like you don't *fit in* anywhere.

Mental

You don't care about family and focus only on yourself and your immediate life. Because you've lost a sense of family connection, you may think nothing matters and become apathetic about the future.

Spiritual

You lose a connected sense of awareness with yourself and the greater connection with your ancestry of origin.

## When the Energy of This Room Is Flowing

You feel connected to the family currently in your life You know that you are the culmination of the physical characteristics and cultural traditions of all those who have come before you, and you find ways to honor that in some way. We have evolved from the Neanderthal man to the unique sophistication of modern mankind, with all its quirks and nuances. You understand this ancestral connection and embrace this aspect of yourself.

## How to Keep the Energy of This Room Flowing

<u>Physical</u>

> ➤ Attend family functions and use this opportunity to learn something new about your family.
> ➤ Keep an icon or two of something that represents your heritage and give it a place of honor.
> ➤ Embrace the family characteristics that are unique to you!

<u>Emotional</u>

> ➤ Express love to the members of your family.
> ➤ Love yourself, because you were purposefully born into your family and a purpose which includes that connection.
> ➤ Find ways to appreciate the love that has been passed down to you.

<u>Mental</u>

> ➤ Know that you have value—because you're here!
> ➤ Sit down with family elders to hear stories of their life.

➤ Find groups that celebrate your same culture or ethnicity. Read books that help you understand your history.

## Spiritual

➤ Give thanks for your family and the ancestral connections.

➤ Spend time with your elders. These people have a lot of wisdom and some are very happy to share that with you!

➤ Read books that speak about spiritual traditions that have been practiced throughout the ages.

# Opportunity

*Opportunity is missed by most people because it is dressed in overalls and looks like work.*

- Thomas A. Edison

*Some of our important choices have a time line. If we delay a decision, the opportunity is gone forever. Sometimes our doubts keep us from making a choice that involves change. Thus an opportunity may be missed.*

- James E. Faust

As we move out into the world, we look for opportunities that will help us be the productive member of society that we were told we should be by our parents and teachers. Opportunities come in all directions, shapes and sizes, from a scholarship for continuing education to finding a mentor who offers us our first job. It's here that we look around to discover what's available to help us achieve the life we want.

The key here is to keep a broader perspective on how you see your life unfolding. Opportunities for what you want show up in all sort of ways, and expectations can slow you down because you're focused on finding something only one way. You can become discouraged if what you want doesn't come in exactly the way you planned it. Sometimes, when we get out of the way of our expectations, something even better comes along! So instead of a specific expectation, think of what you want as a *vision* or *template*. There may really be nothing better than the way you want to have it, but by holding a vision and then be open to looking at alternative avenues for it to show up, you'll be even more sure because you've probably found things you *don't* want.

An example is shopping for a new outfit. You go to the store where you expect to find what you want and then buy what's there. It may not be exactly what you're looking for, but it will do because it's the store you're familiar with. But then you may be disappointed if you walk into another store and discover they carried something even better! Sometimes it helps to *shop around* or get a second opinion because the best opportunity may not be the first place you go. This is where intuition comes in handy; it's a tool that can guide you to the best feeling place or situation.

## The Opportunity of Money

Having money may give us more freedom to have and do the things we want, but those who go for the money alone miss out on other opportunities that money can't buy. We've all heard, and maybe even experienced, the truth that money doesn't buy happiness. Money may open up new opportunities, but it can bring in a whole different set of challenges as well. A wealthy person with ill health would pay a lot of money to regain their health, and many do.

Money in itself is just a form of energy, a tool that's used for trade. We trade money for food and things we need in life. Before money became the modicum of buying and selling, people traded things of value such as livestock and food from their harvest. The adage, "money is the root of all evil" is not true. It is *the love of money*—in other words, the attachment to money—that is the culprit. We all know the story of the miser Scrooge, who learned that the love of money can make for a very lonely life. Money is a tool that comes along naturally as a result of flowing with the energy of *abundance*, but money itself is not a measure of true abundance.

## The Energy of Abundance

As you may have gathered, this room of opportunity is also about abundance, which is much more than just money. Abundance is an *attitude*, a feeling you get when you're filled up to overflowing with the energy of life. It can show up as love, appreciation or joy, and it's a feeling that opens doors to opportunities that may bring in money.

What you think about often comes about. It doesn't matter if you say, "I don't want to get sick!" because you're still focused on sickness. If your thoughts are focused on how much you *don't* have, you'll continue to not have it because that's what you're focused on. In the world of energy, negative words such as *no, not, can't, don't* do not matter because it's all about where you put your attention. Shift your focus to how abundant you feel when you *do* finally have what you want. That will be the energy that you'll attract, because your focus is on feeling abundance, not lack. In the world of energy, you must match the energy of what you want before it can actually come to you. This is what is known as the Law of Attraction; your energy or thoughts attract exactly the same energy you're focused on. Find ways to *feel* abundant to draw abundance—and opportunities—to you!

## Responsibility and Choices

I like to think of the word *responsibility* as our ability to respond—response-ability. We all have the ability to respond, yet many times what we do is react to an outside situation. By taking responsibility for our own thoughts, words and actions, we're able to respond to every situation as it is, not reacting because it's not how we think it should be.

Even though you think the world shows you otherwise, you are never a victim. At every point there is a *choice* to be made. The choice you make becomes either an opportunity or hindrance, because it determines your next steps. Some choices are much harder to make than others, of course, but if you look back on events in your life, you'll see that it all came down to the choices you made. You are responsible for the situations presented to you (because you attract them). You make a decision by choosing one of the options in front of you, which gives you the opportunity to experience the results of that choice.

It does no good to judge yourself harshly for the choices you made, because you made the ones that felt best at that time. None of us purposely make a wrong choice, but we may be cavalier about it by not looking at all the repercussions that could result from that choice, so we may be faced with consequences we didn't intend or desire. Taking responsibility and owning the fact that we made the choices that brought on those consequences helps a lot in getting through them.

## Living with What IS

We're more than happy to take credit or responsibility for the *good* decisions we've made, not so much for the *bad* ones. But in the realm of energy there is no good or bad—everything just *is what it is*. In terms of energy, everything is totally neutral. It's only our label or judgment of something that determines how we experience it.

Consider a hurricane that rips through a city, causing massive destruction and loss of lives. We would say this is a very bad thing, but from the perspective of nature, on the level of energy that just IS, it's simply a huge weather pattern moving across the Earth that happened to travel through a city in its path. Nature just does what it does, and it doesn't take into consideration that we may be affected by it. It's up to us to take appropriate action based on nature's patterns.

Think of your life as a network or web of lines that crisscross each other. At every intersection where these lines cross, you see what IS and you have a choice to make. Do you continue ahead, do you change directions and go left or right or do you stay where you are? Going left will bring different experiences than going right, as will continuing straight ahead. Even deciding to stay where you are offers unique experiences that are different from ones that would have come by taking other directions.

When you're faced with several opportunities, one may look better than another, but it's always the choice we make that determines the experience of what follows, and it is this choice that we're responsible for. If you chose a job where you ended up being unhappy, you may regret that choice. But at the time you made it, you felt it was a good opportunity to get ahead. So instead of wallowing in regret and frustration, simply make another choice: to either stay where you are, try to shift your perspective to be ok with it, or look for something else.

This is another great reason for listening to your inner guidance, because therein is your higher overall perspective. The phrase, *you can't see the forest for the trees* is true when you're in the midst of a circumstance, but your intuition has the view of the whole forest. It's like an inner compass to help you move through it in a direct way.

## The Gift of Challenge

The most successful people on the planet—those who are considered to be a success in all areas of their life— understand self-responsibility. They don't blame others for their struggles. They don't blame the boss who fired them or the spouse who divorced them. By taking full responsibility for their part in challenges, they're able to see them as learning opportunities and use them as steppingstones to have more success in their lives.

It's insightful and meaningful to look back at what happened as a result of a *bad* experience in your life and find a way to see the good that came as a result of it. Because you were fired from that job, you were free to find an even better one. That divorce put you on the path to find a partner who is now the love of your life. Anyone who has had challenges in his or her life (and who hasn't?) will say it's those very challenges that helped make them who and what they are today. It's the butterfly's struggle to break out of its cocoon that strengthens its wings. Without that struggle, the butterfly would be too weak to fly. So it is with our challenges in life—we become stronger for having come through them. By taking responsibility and dealing with what comes to us, we become stronger and wiser.

Every event is an opportunity to learn something about yourself. If you take responsibility for *all* the opportunities (sometimes labeled as challenges) in your life, personal growth will be the result. When you face challenges head-on, you come through to the other side of them wiser and "richer" for having had them. Moving ahead in life begins by taking responsibility for the choices you've made.

## The Value of Living in This Room

The world offers us a wide diversity of opportunities, but it's up to us to choose the ones that make the most sense and feel the best that match the vision we hold for our future. Taking responsibility for the development of your own future empowers you to make better choices. The more you look *outside the box* to find opportunities that may not be right in front of you, the larger your world becomes and the greater the field of opportunities are available to you. As you let go of expectations of how, when, and where you'll find that lucky four-leaf clover, you may discover that it's growing in the field next to you.

## If the Energy of This Room Is Not Flowing

Physical
The systems of your body don't function well and you become *ill at ease*. You experience physical blockages and may think your body is turning against you. If you refuse to take responsibility for your own health, the body will eventually get sick.

Emotional
You feel lethargic or even depressed, frustrated and even angry because you think the world is out to get you, seeing only a hard life ahead.

Mental
You think you're a victim of circumstances, that nobody understands you. You blame others, or your circumstances, for your lack of opportunities.

Spiritual
You blame God for your challenges, saying God doesn't care and never listens, God never answers your prayers. You come to believe you're all alone in life.

## When the Energy of This Room Is Flowing

You feel great because your well is full. You see opportunities everywhere and look forward to new experiences. Your vision for your future is clear because you're focused on what you desire most.

## How to Keep the Energy of This Room Flowing

<u>Physical</u>

➤ Join the YMCA or a gym and take exercise classes like Zumba or yoga, to connect with others and increase your own physical energy.

<u>Emotional</u>

➤ Spend time around happy and fulfilled people as much as possible.

➤ Journal about how great you'll feel when you reach your goals in life and bask in the feeling that you are in control of your own happiness.

<u>Mental</u>

➤ Think outside the box when doing online searches for jobs or other positions.

➤ Talk with others who can help you find opportunities that will take you where you want to be.

<u>Spiritual</u>

➤ Shift your perspective from seeing the challenges in your life to seeing the gifts in them—because every challenge comes with a gift inside it, or you wouldn't have the challenge in the first place.

➤ Write down five things you're grateful for at the end of every day.

# Success

*Put your heart, mind and soul into even your smallest acts. This is the secret of success*

- Swami Sivananda

*Success is where preparation and opportunity meet.*

– Bobby Unser

The world defines success as having *made it* in some way. Either someone overcame huge obstacles to be at the top of their game, or they made a lot of money and now own a thriving business, properties, etc. Success is most often described as a crowning achievement that comes as a result of working hard in the greater world.

## Success from the Inside Out

The kind of success this room is about is a *feeling*, not an achievement. You embarked on your journey with a sense of purpose for your life. You've learned much about yourself and your ancestry growing up. You've found opportunities that paved the way to this point. Now that you're ready to be successful, it's time to go within to discover what success means to *you*. If you don't take a look at this now, you could spend a lot of time trying to achieve something that may not even be what you really want! A career or business endeavor may be what you think you should do to be successful, but inside you feel the desire to paint, sculpt, write music, or get married and have three kids! These can all be successful careers, of course, but the point is to go within to discover what success means to you.

We live in a society that views success as having achieved something in the world. Many people are very successful in this way but inside they still feel that something is missing, something they *just can't put their finger on*. It's the inner voice that says, "this is all good, but what about doing what you really love to do?"

The reason for this unease is because the measure of true success is an *inside achievement*. It's not about what you do but how you *feel* about what you do. It's about doing something that gives you a deep sense of personal fulfillment, and this *feeling* of success can only be found within. It's only when you're doing what you really love to do that you feel fulfilled and successful. If the outer world labels you as successful, that might make you feel good on the outside, but if you're doing something you don't really enjoy, you aren't really a *success* at all. Don't listen to anyone else's definition of success. This is for you to define for yourself, and it's based on how you feel inside.

## Doing What You Love to Do

What do you love to do, so much so that you lose yourself in doing it? You look at the time and are surprised to find that hours have passed because you were so involved with what's in front of you. Find out how to have and do that, because that's true success!

Feeling successful begins when you wake up in the morning. If you're doing something you enjoy, you're eager to begin your day because you know you're going to spend it doing something that feels great. Your energy well is filled to overflowing as you spend time happily doing it. Then, you end your day with a deep sense of fulfillment (success) for a day well spent.

Unfortunately, I hear a lot more people complain about their lives than I do those who speak contentedly about how fulfilled and happy they are with what they do.

You may be someone who has to keep working in a job you dislike because it pays the bills and you can't find anything else. The place to start is to simply look at your situation as *what is* and remind yourself that it won't last forever. Believe that new opportunities come along all the time. Give yourself credit for having made this choice to take care of yourself (and that feels good!). Know that you deserve better than to waste so much of your energy on a job you don't even like. Have the courage and determination to go about finding something else.

Find the gifts hidden right where you are. It may be simply that you have income, a car that gets you there, a friendly co-worker. This will help shift your vibration so you can begin to focus on and attract something else. Picture yourself in a position or job that you enjoy doing and how great it will feel to be doing that! See this picture as a template that could include several options. If you put your focus (and energy) on one particular job or position, you're holding on to one specific expectation and may miss other equally good opportunities.

Inner success brings a deep sense of fulfillment and enjoyment, feelings that hold uplifting energy. *Enjoy* is really an action word. When you do something you love, you en-joy it, or express the energy of joy while doing it. Joy is directly related with love. When you're doing something you en-joy, you're expressing the energy of love—and love really *is* the energy that makes the world go 'round!

## *Should* Versus Desire

Get the word *should* out of your thinking. I used to be quite unhappy because I spent a lot of time and energy doing things I *should* and ignoring what I really wanted to do. I didn't consciously realize this was the problem until a counselor pointed it out to me. She said, "Val, quit should'n all over yourself!" I heard her, and I'm a lot happier now that I allow myself to do more of the things I *want* to do.

Thinking we should do or not do something comes only from the mind. Our minds always have thoughts and opinions about what we want to do, and it's the mind that often messes us up. If you have a pure heart's desire to express yourself in some way, don't let your mind tell you you're not good enough or that someone might not approve of your choice. These are simply sabotaging thoughts that hinder you. Follow your heart, because that's where your true success lies!

## Belief Blocks

If you don't think you're successful in your life, take a look at beliefs about success you may be hanging onto. Perhaps a parent instilled a strong work ethic when you were young and you feel guilty because you believe you're not working hard enough. Maybe your parents said they'd pay your way through school only if you became a doctor/attorney/scientist or took over the family business. If you didn't do that and you don't feel successful, you may be holding onto a belief that success equals following your parents' desires for you. Children and young adults often do what their parents want, out of respect or pressure from these first guides and mentors, even though their hearts are longing to do something else.

Schools, and sometimes parents, are notorious for grooming kids, even as early as elementary school, to think about continuing education and a career. As a result, some may feel pressured to *become someone* before they're emotionally or mentally ready to make these kinds of decisions.

You may have felt this pressure and have adopted a belief about the way to be successful, either indoctrinated or learned, that you *should* do the college-to-career route. Just remember, if you follow what someone else thinks is best for you—if you ignore what you really *want* to do—you may still attain the label of success, but you'll never *feel* successful.

A few years ago, I discovered a deep belief that I carried since childhood. My father worked diligently at everything he did. His unspoken philosophy (that I intuited from observing him) was, "you have to put in a good day's work before you can play."

So I grew up to be a very serious adult because I rarely felt like I worked hard enough to deserve to play. It took some deep intuitive introspection, as well as counseling, to help me uncover and shift this indoctrinated belief.

Sometimes we have to uncover and *un-learn* what we've been taught before we can hear what our heart is calling us to do. Sometimes we have to look at the beliefs that were imposed on us in our early years and determine if they're still true for us today.

True and lasting success means doing whatever gives you a personal sense of enjoyment and fulfillment. . . and you are the only one who knows what that is for you.

## The Value of Living in This Room

Knowing your own personal definition of success gives you greater freedom to choose a future that fits you, feels good and feeds your energy. You're not vulnerable to the good intentions of others, as they impose on you their ideas of what success looks like for you. When you're aware of your own desires and follow them, your path to success is clear and bright and you're eager to live it.

## If the Energy of This Room Is Not Flowing

Physical
You have no energy to get out and do anything. You may

become reclusive. You wake up tired and go to bed tired but don't sleep well.

### Emotional

You feel stuck and go emotionally numb to avoid facing your feelings of frustration and hopelessness. You lose your desire to engage in life. Because your life has no meaning, you don't care about doing things that you enjoy.

### Mental

You become frustrated because you're unhappy in your job or career, but you believe you're stuck there because you can't think of any way out. You think "what's the use?"

### Spiritual

You lose your greater sense of purpose and meaning for your life and just go through the motions of working and living.

## When the Energy of This Room Is Flowing

You look forward to a new day because of what it may bring your way. You're happy and have a strong sense of personal fulfillment. You have no need to compare yourself or your life to anyone else. You know that your being in the world makes a difference!

# How to Keep the Energy of This Room Flowing

## Physical

➢ Take a moment when you first wake up to appreciate the good things right where you are.

➢ Find something to wear or carry with you that represents the personal success you've achieved.

## Emotional

➢ Put an icon of your success in a place where you see it often. It's a reminder of your personal achievement and you'll feel great every time you look at it.

➢ Remind yourself often of all the successful things you've accomplished in your life.

## Mental

➢ Make it a point to do something you enjoy or love to do every day, something that is personally fulfilling. This keeps your mind in the habit of true successful thinking.

➢ Look back at something you think you failed at, then examine it for the pieces that were successful. Be grateful that something helped you to move on.

## Spiritual

➢ As you live the deeper purpose of your life, you become a wonderful example and a light for others in the world.

➢ Find something in your life that you are grateful for.

# Relationship

*No one can live without relationship. You may withdraw into the mountains, become a monk, a sannyasi, wander off into the desert by yourself, but you are related. You cannot escape from that absolute fact. You cannot exist in isolation.*

- Jiddu Krishnamurti


*But let there be spaces in your togetherness and let the winds of the heavens dance between you. Love one another but make not a bond of love. Let it rather be a moving sea between the shores of your souls.*

- Kahlil Gibran

This room includes more than a marriage or intimate partnership, or even our immediate or wider family. It's about the way we *relate* to everyone and everything around us. We live in a physical world made up of an abundance of amazingly diverse and unique forms, which gives us ongoing opportunities to *relate* in some way with everything.

Each one of us is physically unique. Even twins have a small feature or two that is different from their twin. We are also unique on the inside, because we think and act in unique ways, having experienced the years of our lives in different ways from any other.

## Relationship in Form

Humans are here to be in relationship—with other people, with the natural and man-made world and with themselves. The world is made up of zillions of unique forms that come in all kinds of shapes, colors and sizes, and each form is in relationship to every other form in some way. Nature wraps itself around us through the sun and rain, trees and flowers. We live with animals in our homes. We've built unique structures called homes and businesses that together make a city. Everything is inter-connected and in relationship.

Because of our unique human differences, we're naturally drawn to and curious about others. You can see this clearly when very young children meet for the first time. They're naturally curious about each other and have an innocent sense of discovery.

We were born to be in relationship. We are born with a gender identity, being either male or female. (I know in today's world these lines sometimes get blurred, but I speak in general terms for the sake of this topic). We were given different bodies specifically to be in relationship with a unique other. This happens on all sorts of levels, from a casual meeting or friendship to sexual union to living together in love.

## Growth in Relating

Relationship is an opportunity to see ourselves as part of a greater whole, to have the awareness that we're part of something called the human race and we have *relatives* who live all over the planet. We all have our likes and dislikes about them, just as we do our close family relatives, but I believe the only way we will be able to thrive as a species is to accept all our relatives around the world, with all their quirks and idiosyncrasies!

People of different cultures sometimes have difficulty relating to and accepting the differences. As I mentioned earlier, the mind has a tendency to label and judge *different* as good or bad, which makes for challenges in finding ways to relate with each other. Most of the countries around the world are in some kind of relationship with each other, based on proximity or need. The world has become a global economy, where one country can have an effect on the prosperity or lack of another. It all depends on their relationship.

When we understand our inter-connection or relationship with everything and everyone, it can help us become more forgiving and compassionate toward everyone, even those who we don't perceive as being "like us." This happens on all levels of relationship, from the entire human race in all its diversity to a person we pass on the street who looks different than us.

As we practice being in relationship with each other, we begin to see how alike we really are from the inside out. The deeper the connection with someone, the more we *relate* to and with them. The whole world is created to be in relationship. Plants, flowers and trees need sun and rain to survive. It takes two to make a baby, and it's now well known that babies suffer and can die without the touch of another. We need each other, and that's a wonderful thing.

## Connecting from the Inside Out

We are all packets of energy in a skin cover. Our energy is always vibrating and moving . . . radiating in, around and through us, so of course our own energy (sometimes called our aura or etheric body) melds with the energy of other people we meet. When this happens, we get an immediate inner sense of the other. Before you ever speak to or touch someone physically, your energy bodies have connected, and you *know* something about them. This is all done in a nano-second and most of the time we aren't even consciously aware of it, yet we get an impression or feeling about the other. If you've ever walked by someone in a store and got the feeling that they were having a bad day, or you met someone for the first time and before you even shake hands or say hello, you *just know* you're going to like them, you've experienced the result of the interaction or blending of your energies.

Every relationship is based on interaction or *connection* with the other, on both the physical and energy levels. You may have a short conversation/connection with a cashier at the grocery store and then go home to a deeper connection with your spouse and your children, and even a pet if you have one. You have a sleeping connection/relationship with the mattress on your bed, and you have a relationship with your breakfast food and utensils the next morning. Relationship is about both the inner and outer *connection* between you and the other. You have a relationship with everyone and *everything* in your life.

As an example of relationship with something, consider sitting down to write a letter. There is a piece of paper, a pen, and your hand. These are three unique forms simply being what they are in their separate and unique forms. When you pick up the pen with your hand, that pen is now in relationship with your hand, and vice versa. When you put the pen onto the paper and begin writing, your hand, the pen and the paper are all in relationship, in energetic connection, with each other, and you now begin to create something greater than the three individual pieces could ever do by themselves.

This is the synergetic, creative power of relationship. In the example of a love relationship between two people, I see this as 1+1=3—put two individuals together and the synergy of the energetic connection between the two creates something greater than those two as individuals could accomplish on their own. The love that is ignited between them is a powerful synergetic force that keeps the relationship alive and thriving. I believe the greatest miracle expressed out of this synergy is the making of another human being.

## The Mirrors in Our Lives

Relationship is a very powerful learning and growth tool. The people we interact with are reflections or *mirrors* to help us see how we're doing. We can't be truly objective about ourselves because we see ourselves only from the perspective of who we think we are, and so we're biased. (We also have a mind that is not at all objective about who we really are.) The psychologist Alan Watts put it humorously when he said we can't bite our own teeth or see our own eyes—we have to look into a mirror to see what we look like, and then we see ourselves backward.

We interact with other people, and in doing so, they show us what we can't see about ourselves. Using the analogy of a mirror, other people reflect back to us what they see and feel about what we're showing or projecting into the world. We are often not aware of what we're projecting, but we can see it from their perspective. They see the *image* we show to them. Their opinions about us may not be what we hold to be true for ourselves, but it certainly is their truth. Just as your truth is the result of the life you've lived, their truth about you comes from their own life perspective. But it's still holds valuable information for you, because they are the mirrors that reflect back to you the *face* you're showing to the world.

Depending on the relationship you have with another, whether it be a co-worker, spouse or even the barista at Starbucks, you have opportunities to learn something about yourself.

For example, a friend says to you, "Wow, you're pretty angry today." Your immediate reaction may be to deny it—you don't think you're angry, you just explained something very calmly, and you think she has a lot of nerve saying that to you! But that friend, that *mirror*, has told (shown) you something that you haven't been able or willing to see about yourself. The truth is, there *is* something going on inside you around the emotion of anger. Your friend senses it, but you blame them—because you're not willing to look inside.

## Thorns and Buttons

In his book *The Untethered Soul*, Michael Singer calls denied feelings *thorns*. Because they're painful when touched, we cover up these thorns with all sorts of justifications—we protect the very thing that is causing us pain, and this takes up a lot of our time and energy!

This is one of the many reasons why relationships are powerful. Others close to you can sense your energy, so at some point they'll touch one of those thorns! You know they have when you lash back at them and vehemently defend yourself. This gives you the great opportunity to pull out that thorn and dig into why you still hang onto something that hurts so much!

We have a saying, "He/she pushes my buttons." You think the other person is the problem, but it's not about them at all. Who has the button? You! The other person is just showing you your button (he pushes *my* buttons!). Instead of blaming them when they do this, understand that he or she is simply pointing out (reflecting) to you that you're in denial of something that's uncomfortable to look at. Now it becomes an opportunity to find out what this button is all about and why you have it in the first place.

Relationships of all kinds are opportunities to learn about ourselves. In a way, relationships help us uncover those parts of ourselves that we think we keep hidden. This is why someone else is considered a mirror. It doesn't mean that being in a relationship is hard or unpleasant or will be a lot of work, but it does mean that there will be more opportunities for growth in them than being on your own. If you really want to speed-up your growth into self-awareness, spend time with people who push your buttons.

## Love is Good Energy

This room of relationship is all about *love*. Love is the energetic force that creates all life. We were created with and from Godness, which is pure love. It's the feeling that originates in the heart, the center that holds our connection to that Godness. You cannot think your way into loving, it's pure feeling. You may have had a relationship you really wanted to work, one in which you *thought* you were in love, but in the end it dissolved. This happened because it wasn't true love from the heart. I've been there and I know the difference.

We have a saying, "my heart's not in it." If you pursue anything feeling like this—a job or career, a move, a relationship—it probably won't work out like you want it to. This relates back to the room of Success: if you take a job you know you won't like (your heart's not in it) but you take it anyway, it will drain your energy because you don't enjoy it or bring the energy of love to it. We need to feel the energy of love to live a happy life, so it's very important to do things we love and enjoy—keep that well filled!

There's a saying, "love makes the world go 'round." This is so true! Love is an expansive energy that needs to be expressed and shared. Loving is energy in motion. Look around you—the trees, flowers, grasses, mountains, birds, animals, sky, sun, moon—everything, including us, was created with the energy of love. When you see the true beauty of the Earth, you are seeing expressions of love, the energy of creation, in form.

When I look closely at a flower, I'm amazed at the beautiful intricacy of it, and I think about the great amount of love that must have gone into creating such a thing. Can you even imagine how much fun the Creator, the source of love, must have had to design a whole world of such amazing diversity?

All you have to do is look at an ostrich to know that the Creator also had a sense of humor.

We've come to think that "being in love" is something that happens only with certain significant people in our lives, but this puts a limitation on the true energy of love. When we are loving and living in and with the energy of love, our own energy expands and our well fills. Our aura grows and others can feel that expansiveness. Love is palpable when it's expressed freely, and those who *live in love* are a joy to connect with. This is how we feel when we're in love with life.

Has someone ever told you "I love you"—but it just didn't feel true to you? They said the words but there was no energy of love behind it. A minister once told me that love is a verb, and I believe that's true. This is why loving actions like a hug feel so good; a hug is an active *expression* of love and can mean so much more than just words.

You may have read the book *The 5 Love Languages* by Gary Chapman. He says there are five different ways to express love, and we can rate these according to how we best want to receive love. Knowing what someone's highest love language is helps you to show your love for them in a way that feels best to them.

## The Value of Living in This Room

As you become more aware of your own relationship with yourself, as you love yourself just as you are, with all your so-called imperfections, you shift your focus from self to other.

Because you feel good about yourself, you're free to form relationships with other people. You see every person you're in relationship with as a valuable piece in your life puzzle, and you come to know that your life wouldn't be complete without each of them.

## If the Energy of This Room Is Not Flowing

Physical

You experience challenges in your relationships and have difficulty maintaining them. You have little desire to be around others and can become isolated in your life.

Emotional

You feel sadness and despair. You blame others, saying that they just don't get you, and you become angry at life in general.

Mental

You think it's easier to be alone than face the challenges you've heard about that happen in any kind of relationship. You think you're better off avoiding uncomfortable situations.

Spiritual

You may become an atheist or agnostic. Because you have no relationship with yourself or with Godness, you have no sense of the true meaning of love and can become apathetic about life.

## When the Energy of This Room Is Flowing

Because you see the greater meaning and purpose of love, you love to share it with others and you're a joy to be around. You are light and happy, peaceful and content with your life as it is . . .because you love it!

## How to Keep the Energy of This Room Flowing

Physical

➢ Honor your body, because living inside it is the most intimate relationship you have. It's with you every second of your life.
➢ Love it by doing things to keep it healthy and strong, like regular exercise, eating healthy foods and plenty of rest.
➢ Say something pleasant to the checkout person at the grocery store, and other people you encounter in your day. You may just help to make their day brighter.

Emotional

➢ Take the time to uncover thorns and buttons because you love yourself too much to hang onto things that hurt you.
➢ Spend time with people you love and give love in return.

Mental

➢ Think of ways to express love.

> ➢ Tell someone you appreciate something about them.
> ➢ Send thank you notes and get-well cards via snail mail—because it's fun to receive a note in the mailbox!

## Spiritual

> ➢ Spend time in spiritual settings like a church or other holy building where the energy of love can be felt.
> ➢ Spend time in the creation of nature to deepen your sense of connection and relationship with all of life.

# Creativity

*True creativity often starts where language ends.*

                    - Arthur Koestler

*Creativity is an energy. It's a precious energy, and it's something to be protected. A lot of people take for granted that they're a creative person, but I know from experience, feeling it in myself, it is a magic, it is an energy. And it can't be taken for granted.*

                    - Ava DuVernay

Because we as humans were created from the ultimate creative source, we are born with the ability to be *creative*. The word *human* is really two words, Hu-Man: Hu, meaning the spark of life energy or Godness, and Man as the physical aspect. We are truly God and Man, having both energies within us. This means that we are created beings and we have the ability to be creative.

Our deepest urge is to express that creative energy because it's an innate part of who we are, having been created ourselves. Young children are naturally creative and will make up all sorts of games and scenarios without being coached on how to do it. Look at any refrigerator door in a household with children and it's probably filled with their creative expressions.

## Creativity in Action

We are only fully alive when we express this aspect of who we are in some way. In some people, creative expression is a definite drive, while in others it feels like something fun to do occasionally. Galleries, theaters and concert halls are filled with artists who were driven to express their creative side and then offer it to the world. This drive also shows up in architecture, technology and medicine. Children love to draw and color, rebellious kids paint graffiti on walls, and inventors have the creative vision to see and make something new and unique.

Nature is an amazing example of creativity in action. Each season brings beautiful expressions of Nature having fun.

After the hibernation of winter, Nature explodes in its creative expression with new life and continues right on through fall; even the turning again toward winter and hibernation is beautiful, with the vibrant colors of leaves before they fall. It's said that each snowflake is unique—talk about an amazing creative expression!

## Expressing Life Creatively

On the cycle of the rooms of our life, this is the point where we feel the desire to express all we've learned from our life experiences. Some people take art or dance classes, learn a new skill or hobby, make jewelry, a scrapbook or flower arrangements. There is no right or wrong here, it's all about finding ways to express that innate creative desire.

Our creative expressions come from desire. The world is filled with the results of this desire, from clothing, cars and furniture to the latest technological advances. The human desire to create something never ends, because we never run out of ideas!

It's very important to express this innate desire to be creative because it's what we're born to do. Paint, draw, play, cook something and simply get lost in the fun of doing it! Does it really matter if anyone else sees or hears it? Because your creative expressions are uniquely your own, there can be no judgment or labels about them. If someone doesn't like your painting, for instance, it's simply how *they* see it and has nothing to do with you. You've spent time-out-of-time getting lost in doing something you love, expressing your deep desire to create—and that's what truly matters.

If I had let the thought that some people would judge this book stop me from getting it published, it would not be in your hands right now. I would have given into that fear (the mind's fear) and then deprived others who would enjoy it and benefit from it. I had to let go of all fear and doubt—tell the mind to shut up! —and publish it simply because I could not *not* do so.

People will always like some creative expressions and not others. This is not a judgment of the artist's work, but simply their preference. I may not like certain pieces of art in a gallery, but I can still appreciate the creative expression of that artist. A gallery is filled with many different and unique expressions because there are many different and unique people.

I'm also appreciative of the creative people who build the unique galleries, theaters, restaurants and other structures that house so many different creative expressions. They have the vision to see that the world is a better place when we have opportunities to view creativity in action.

## Imagination

Children are the embodiment of *play* and they have huge imaginations. They imagine whole scenarios where they act out imaginary characters. When I was a kid, my sister and I raked leaves to make paths that we called roads and we drove (on our bikes) from one imaginary house to another. In the winter after a big snowfall, we couldn't wait to go outside and make caves in the snowdrifts that became our houses. We would visit each other, just like the grownups did!

Every creative expression begins with an idea that often just *comes to us*. As my feng shui teacher Carol said, imagination means to *image in* an idea. I asked her, what if I'm just making it up? She said, of course you're making it up—that's what imagination is!

Many artists will tell you that their art *came through* them. The desire to be creative comes from our innate connection with our creative source. The creative urge then *begins to form* as an image or idea in our mind, and it's up to us whether we take it into a physical form or not. So many adults have lost their imaginative ability simply because they don't practice using their imagination.

If you don't use it, you'll lose it. Even reading a book is using your imagination in a small way, because you imagine putting yourself into the story. Daydreaming isn't a waste of time, it's a way to practice using imagination. Watch the movie, *The Secret Life of Walter Mitty* and you'll understand the fun and value of using your imagination!

I am simply amazed at some of the animated movies that are out these days . . . so imaginative and fun to watch high levels of creativity in action! Disney World and Disneyland are wonderful products of imagination and creative expression.

Walt Disney and his team of Imagineers (yes, that's what they're called!) have made whole careers using their imaginations to create a place where millions come to play. Through the years, teams of Imagineers have continued to create an ongoing and timeless expression that is truly mind-boggling!

As adults, we tend to think that being playful is silly, something we've outgrown—like silliness is a bad thing. But the really bad thing is when we *stop* being silly sometimes. Adult humans are the only ones who suppress their natural desire to play. Children love it when the adults play with them, and often, if we allow ourselves to play, we have as much fun as the kids! I think this is why it's such fun being a grandparent—you have an excuse to play with the kids and act silly! If you don't have children in your life, find ways to express your *inner child*, that part you that never grows old and is always looking for ways to play, no matter how old you are!

Animals love to play at any age. If you've ever seen an old arthritic cat chase a toy mouse, or an old dog chase a ball, you understand that play is a natural instinct for every species throughout their life span. Play and creative expression are not only fun but are also very good for us. Allowing our inner child to create and be silly helps us stay young at heart.

Children should never be criticized for their creativity. Giving a child anything less than an A in art class can dampen and even shut down their creative ability. I remember making a vase in pottery class in fourth grade. Even though it didn't turn out the way I envisioned it, I was pretty proud of it. But the teacher gave me a C, and from that I took the unspoken message—not only was I not good enough to be a potter, I'd never be an artist. When I brought it home, though, Mom put flowers in it and placed it on a hall table, which helped to revive my squashed creative desire. I still don't think I'm artistic—but you're reading a book that's the result of my desire to express my creativity through writing!

## The Cycle of an Idea

A wholistic life can be viewed as a birth-to-death cycle, beginning with birth in the Center, moving around the wheel or cycle, and then returning to the Center at death. This metaphor can also be used to understand the creative cycle of an inspired idea.

Say you have a great idea for a new product, an inspiration that begins with an Aha! moment. The inspiration comes to you from the Center, from your heart connection, and then the mind takes this idea and runs with it, beginning the *life path* of this idea. You become aware of its value, not only for yourself (you could make money!) but also because it may have value for the *family* of man, which continues the cycle.

Then, as you develop this idea, you look for *opportunities* such as funding or partners to make the idea a reality. When the idea becomes a *success*, you now have a thriving *relationship* with it. You then find *creative* ways to develop and market it.

Finally, you've gained *wisdom* from all the experiences you had related to your idea, and you then share it with the people who will benefit from it. Your creative and developmental work is done, but the benefit lives on.

## The Value of Living in This Room

When we express our innate desire to be creative, we honor the gift of our own creation as a human being. When we *receive* inspiration from our heart connection and then express that into some kind of form, we *give back* the energy that we are made of. It's only when we take action to create something from the inspiration we've received that keeps this energy flowing. The continuous cycle of *receive-and-give* brings a sense of meaning and fulfillment to our life.

## If the Energy of This Room Is Not Flowing

Physical
Your body feels like something you drag around with you. You don't care about how you look or what you wear, and shopping for gifts becomes a chore.

Emotional
You feel antsy. There is an urge inside that you suppress because you don't know how, or refuse, to express it. You become frustrated because nothing you do feels good.

Mental

You experience *writer's block* in life and can't think of anything fun or creative to do. You're afraid to try anything new or different out of fear you may not be good enough.

Spiritual

Nothing you see or do inspires you. You lose your sense of seeing the beauty all around you, and your life is something to get through day to day.

## When the Energy of This Room Is Flowing

You have lots of creative life-enhancing energy and can imagine all sorts of ways to express it. You're happy and fulfilled because you live with the flow of creation. Because you express your creativity, your well is full and you're a joy to be around. People love to see what you've done!

## How to Keep the Energy of This Room Flowing

Physical

➢ Take dance or yoga classes, do something that gets the body moving in creative ways.
➢ Wear fun clothes that express how you feel.
➢ Go play at an amusement park.

## Emotional

- ➢ Go to an art gallery. Sit in front of a piece of art that inspires you. Imagine being the artist who created it, from their initial steps to the finished product. Putting yourself in their shoes helps to feel admiration and have compassion for their effort, and this can feel very good.
- ➢ Put on some music and feel the rhythm pulsing through you, urging you to move with it—and then let yourself do it!

## Mental

- ➢ Go to a craft store and immerse yourself in all the creative ideas there. If nothing else, get a coloring book and crayons and have fun!
- ➢ If you like to doodle, try doing Zen Tangles.

## Spiritual

- ➢ Connect often with the Creator for inspiration.
- ➢ Pray, ask for inspirational ideas, then listen for what comes to you.
- ➢ Spend time in nature, the most amazing creation we had nothing to do with.

# Wisdom

*I've had a life that has taken many interesting paths. I've learned a lot from mentors who were instrumental in shaping me, and I want to share what I've learned.*

- Herbie Hancock

*Thousands of candles can be lighted from a single candle, and the life of the candle will not be shortened. Happiness never decreases by being shared.*

- Buddha

This is the last room on the cycle of your life. It's the culmination of all your experiences and the wisdom you gained from what you've learned as a result of living them. It's here that you share this wisdom with others so they may benefit from what you've come to know.

I like to think of wisdom as the end result of experiences. You live through an experience and something happens as a result. If you look at whatever you experienced from the perspective that you learned something about yourself from it, and then dig inside to discover what that is, you gain wisdom. Experience + learning + new self-awareness = wisdom.

## The Value of Experience

We live through a multitude of experiences during the course of our lives. Many people think of them as just part of living or they don't think about them at all. But every experience has value. There's a purpose, a reason why we lived it or we wouldn't have had that experience in the first place. The reason could be as simple as a reminder to appreciate where you are, or it could be as complex as losing a job, divorce or the death of a loved one. No matter what level of experience you go through, there is always something to take away from it that helps you understand yourself, and sometimes others as well, on a deeper level. The thing to remember is, the experience is for you, and there is always something in it for you.

Life on this physical realm is not an accident, there's a reason why we're here, and I believe that every experience is a *gift* (sometimes in disguise) to help us understand that reason. But we have to look at it from this perspective to see the purpose and the gift.

## We Are Actors in the Theater of Life

A famous quote from Shakespeare's play *As You Like It* reads, "All the world's a stage, and all the men and women merely players; they have their exits and their entrances…"

I believe Shakespeare was writing about a deep truth that came to him as an inspiration. As I alluded to earlier, I believe we come into physical form to play or act out a script that we designed, a script that has many different roles acted out by all the many people in our lives. We play these roles together to have various experiences so we can learn more about who we are.

Another quote that relates to this idea of learning from our experiences is from Richard Bach's book *Illusions*, which says "Every person, all the events of your life are there because you have drawn them there. What you choose to do with them is up to you."

## My Own Wisdom Experience

Because I believe that I can learn something from every one of my experiences, I decided to do an intensive study of my life. I wanted to see if I could figure out what I learned. So, in the fall of 2016, I took a pen and paper and started to write down as many experiences as I could remember, beginning with the year I was born. I wrote them in five-year increments, up to the current day I was writing. I didn't remember many in the first five years, but when I was done, I'd written out 20 pages of various things I'd lived through in the years of my life.

Then I went back and wrote down what I thought I'd learned from each experience—which was a real eye-opener! The last step I took was to go over the list of what I thought I'd learned, but this time from the perspective of love and acceptance, from knowing there was a gift in every one of those experiences.

It took me several days to get through all those years of experiences and find the gifts they offered. There were many emotional moments, both happy and sad. I could see that there were things I did that turned out to be catalysts that got me to the next level of understanding my life, and some so small they hardly mattered. There were experiences that I treasured and those I regretted. It was a roller-coaster of emotions, but I knew deep down that I was doing something very important, so stayed with it.

After I was finished, I put the pages together in a special folder and made a creative cover for it. When I took away all the mind's thoughts about comparing my life to anyone else's, I discovered that I'd lived a very enriching and valuable life. I came away with a profound appreciation of and love for myself and the amazing synchronicities—some I'd now consider miracles—that had to happen for me to be exactly where I was. Of course, this exercise will continue as long as I'm here, as I keep learning from my ongoing experiences. It's difficult to put into words, but I now can see that I've gained *wisdom,* because I know the purpose of my experiences. I highly recommend this exercise for anyone who wants to see the wisdom gained from their own experiences.

## A New Look at Life

If you're in the beginning or middle phases of your life, this room is about taking your self-awareness to another level. Wisdom is not something that's gained toward the end of a life, it can be realized at every step of the way, after every experience. I didn't realize this until I'd lived many years, but I see now, had I had the self-awareness to look at each one my experiences and learn from them as I lived them, I could have saved myself a lot of headaches and heartaches along the way.

Wisdom comes to the one who's had the experience, and then can be shared with others. As you come to know more about who you are and what you desire to be, do, and have, you now take this wisdom with you as you step back into the room of Life Path. Using this wisdom as you continue on through another cycle through the rooms of your life, you're able to make wiser choices in your experiences.

## The Retirement Experience

Heading into the experience of retirement can be a winding down from the chaos of the work-world, a time to simply enjoy the remaining years to travel and do the things you didn't get to do before because you were so busy working. Retirement can also be an isolating time where you lose your sense of connection to the world. Your closest friends may have been the people you worked with; your social activities may have been with these friends, or within the network of your career. In retirement, all these relationships and activities may fade away, bringing on a sense of loss. If this loss doesn't shift and if new relationships and new activities aren't developed, depression and even physical illness may be the result.

Many retired people find places to volunteer as a way to stay involved and connected. Others find a hobby that keeps them interested. Some join groups that have special interests, such as book clubs or birdwatching.

No matter how you do it, it's important at this time in life to do something to stay connected and not completely drop out of the world. Even more important, this is a time to give back what you've gained. The energy of this room is about sharing the wisdom you've gained from your life experiences.

AARP is an advocacy agency designed to help seniors (50 and over) stay in touch and connected. It does a great job of stressing the need to stay connected and offers real-life examples of people who have found ways to do that. In addition to helping seniors understand how to manage their financial, health, and home life in retirement, AARP highlights inspirational examples of retired people who have found a way to do what they love to do and even turn it into a business. The organization is also a good resource for locating groups and communities of like-minded people to connect with.

## The Wisdom of Elders

You may be of an age when you've become the *elder*, the concept that was mentioned in the room of Family. It's important now, as the elder in your family, to share your wisdom with them. You're embarking upon the phase which leads eventually to becoming one of the ancestors. This is the time to consider leaving your *legacy* for future generations.

If you are an elder, this room is the last one on the life cycle, where you prepare for your transition to go back to the Center. You've lived what is considered a whole life, you've had all kinds of amazing experiences and it's time to gather all the energy of all the rooms into one great bundle of wisdom, a legacy that you not only leave behind for the benefit of future generations, but wisdom that you take with you when you leave.

When the body *dies* (it doesn't really die, it only transforms back into other energies), who you really are—a spark of Godness—moves on to an unknown *something*. This is something or somewhere that we, in our little bodies with our little minds, cannot even conceive of, and there are many different ideas about what that might be. We do, however, have a sense, an inner knowing, that there is *something else* beyond this one life. Some, as I do, believe we come back here again and again—reincarnation. Some believe we live this one life and then go *Home*, whatever that is to the one who holds that belief. Some believe we continue on to other realms to have other experiences. All are possibilities, and all are true for the ones who hold that belief. Can you look at these different possibilities without judgment, believing there are different ways of looking at what happens to us at the end of our lives?

## The Individuality of Belief

Each of us holds our own truth based on what we believe; it's something that sustains us on our life journey. Because none of us knows for sure the truth of what's really going to happen when we leave the body, belief is an individual thing. What's true for one may not be true for another, and this is just the way *it is*.

When people come together to share in a like belief, a congregation is formed and a building, sometimes called a church, may be built for those people to come together in worship. There are many different churches and spiritual centers around the world, with as many different beliefs about life and death. Each one is to be respected for what it is because it's their belief and their truth, just as yours is your truth.

We're all on our own personal and unique life journey, and if what we believe sustains us and gives meaning and purpose to our lives, that's all that matters. What I believe may not be what someone else believes, but if you and I are both happy in our beliefs and we respect each other, we'll get along. After all, the whole point of being here is to be happy, and every person goes about creating that in their own unique way. We are unique in how we express our humanity—but we are all humans, one species sharing the same planet. This is what makes the cycle of life so very interesting!

## Legacy

I saw a Facebook post recently that read, "Don't die with the music in your head!" I think this is a beautiful way to express the importance of leaving a legacy.

One of the definitions of legacy in the dictionary is *something transmitted by or received from an ancestor or predecessor or from the past.* I want you to think of the totality of your life as a legacy, a gift you offer to loved ones.

My mother and father died with their legacy untold. Yes, they probably shared stories with us at various times, but nothing was put into form. I wish I'd asked them to tell me about their lives so I could learn about them as a woman and a man, not just Mom and Dad. I'm sure I could have learned a lot, not only about them but myself as well. They probably learned valuable lessons that I could have used as tools to help me make better decisions in my own life. Because they're gone now, much of their wisdom, their music, has gone with them.

Making a written or verbal record of the "music" of your life for your loved ones is a wonderful gift, not only for their enjoyment but for your own, as you share your wisdom with them. There are several ways to do this. Simply telling your stories to the family is fine, but getting them on paper or voice-recorded is much better, because this physical record can be passed down to future generations. If the idea of writing or recording doesn't feel pleasurable to you, there are people who are in the business of helping elders record their legacy.

Many cultures around the world revere their elders. In these cultures, they aren't just old people but are wise ones who have lived through many experiences. They are asked to share what are sometimes called the *wisdom stories* that can be so valuable to younger generations. The young ones know they can learn things that may help them avoid challenges, *because* the elders have already faced them and learned from the experience. Unfortunately, this attitude is not held around the world. Maybe it's time for us to begin to think about the culture of eldering in our own lives.

## The Value of Living in This Room

So often people at this stage of their lives look back on their lives with regret or frustration because of things they either did or didn't do. This takes away energy needed for living in the present and planning for the future.  When you're aware of the value of *every* experience you've had in your life, you can let go of regret. Doing a life review of some sort will help you connect the dots from one event to another to see the overall journey that is your life path, and its value for you.

## If the Energy of This Room Is Not Flowing

Physical
You have no energy to get out and do anything or see anyone and may become isolated and alone, just waiting out your last years.

Emotional
You feel lonely and may become depressed, with a feeling that nobody cares about you anymore.

Mental
You think that everyone else is having fun and you get resentful. You look back at your life with regret for all the things you could have done but didn't, but you think it's too late to start anything new now.

Spiritual
You've lost faith in yourself and your connection to Godness

and fear dying. You live with the hope that there's something better after you die.

## When the Energy of This Room Is Flowing

You feel younger than your chronological age and enjoy doing things with other people. You have plans for the future and stay focused on the present moment, knowing it's all you have!

## How to Keep the Energy of This Room Flowing

<u>Physical</u>

> ➤ Get out and do fun things with other people.
> ➤ Join a card or game club or volunteer at a place where you feel supported and can make a difference.
> ➤ Spend time with your family sharing stories together.
> ➤ Play with children.

<u>Emotional</u>

> ➤ Write down all the gifts of things and people that have come your way throughout your life.
> ➤ Spend time doing things you enjoy doing, both with other people and on your own.
> ➤ Do something creative and be an inspiration to others.

## Mental

- ➢ Buy a notebook and pen and begin a legacy journal, even if it's just notes. Carry this with you, and every time you think of something in your past, write it down. This is the beginning of creating your legacy.
- ➢ Reconnect with someone who made a difference in your life and let them know the impact they had on you when you were younger.

## Spiritual

- ➢ Visit holy places that bring you a sense of Wholeness to your life.
- ➢ More than ever, it's important to connect with Godness, because you're getting closer to Home – and that's a wonderful thing!

# The House
# That Is Your Life

*We might not be the ones to change the world. We might not belong to the few that "put a ding in the universe." We might not be something the whole world would celebrate. But, in the little corners that we live, in the lives we've played a part in, we should be nothing but unforgettable.*

- Nesta Jojoe Erskine

Life is a cycle made up of numerous rooms, and as such it needs to flow. As we've learned, each of these nine rooms plays a part in achieving and maintaining the balance and flow of a complete or wholistic life. Ignore one room and the others suffer in some way. Ignore it long enough and your whole life can become compromised.

## The Energy of a Wholistic Life

The underlying theme of this metaphor of life as a house with nine rooms is energy. We live in a physical world made up of forms, but these forms are simply the visible representations of the energy that makes up those forms. When we go through life viewing it only on the surface, paying attention to only what we view with our five physical senses, we miss out on a whole inner world, with its wealth of opportunities to help us see the deeper aspects of who we really are. Just like there's a whole different world beneath the surface of the ocean, there's a whole different world beneath the surface of our lives—so why not explore this part as well?

We bring our own energy into each *room* to live out some piece of our life. The more energy we have available to put into a room, the better it feels. Because feeling good makes more good energy, there is more energy available for the next room on the cycle. A slowdown or blockage of energy in one room blocks available energy for the next room. If the center of our life is stifled, it affects all the other parts of our life, because the center gets its energy from Godness, the ultimate energy source.

## The Wholistic Source

You might understand this concept of source energy by looking at electricity. Electricity is generated or created from a main power plant or generator—a source. The massive amount of electric energy created here needs to be downgraded in intensity and power many times before it ever reaches the outlets in our homes. The electricity goes through transformers, transistors or resistors to slow it down and decrease the flow of electricity so that we don't get blown up when we turn on a light. Each house has an electrical panel where a larger amount of electricity comes in from the street and is diverted into various rooms. On the panel are switches called circuit breakers, which are designed to break or stop the flow of electricity if it overloads the capacity of that wire.

The same is true for life energy. It begins at a source that is beyond our understanding because it's just so huge. This intense and rapid vibrational flow of energy gets slowed way down into the energy that holds physical form. By the time energy becomes physical, its vibration has slowed down into a vibrational form that our physical brains interpret as something. The slower the vibration, the denser the energy. A rock is energy moving at a very slow rate.

## Energy Flow Determines the Flow of Our Life

Just like electricity, we can shut off the flow of energy. When we turn off a lamp, the room goes dark because the energy has stopped flowing. The same is true with our life. If we *unplug* from our energy source, we cut off the flow to that room, and a part of our life gets out of balance. Then there isn't enough energy available to flow through the cycle, into the other areas of our life. This isn't something to fear, but it's good to know. The flow of energy *lights* our life, it allows us to keep going. Keep the energy flowing and it will help you be the light in your life!

We know the amount of energy we bring to our life by how we *feel* about it. Feelings are wonderful indicators of the direction we're headed. Basically, if it doesn't feel good, it's probably not a good idea. So often we dismiss feelings in favor of the mind. We think if something makes sense, that's good enough. But we ignore feelings at our own peril.

## Living Whole-Heartedly

There's an important reason why we humans have both a heart and a mind. Basically, we connect with Godness through the heart to receive the energy of love and inspiration, and we use the mind to bring this love and these inspirations into our physical life to *furnish* the rooms that make up that life.

This is the concept of *whole-heartedness*. We need both the heart and the mind as we make our way as human beings. All the problems we encounter are the result of an imbalance in this whole-heartedness. As a human race, we've become overly focused on the mind and our outer physical world, and there is mounting evidence of this in just about every corner of the world.

The mind is with us only while we're in body, so its main concern is with keeping us safe and helping us accomplish things on the physical level. Ideally, it is instrumental in helping us fulfill our desires on the physical level by guiding us to the people, places and things that can make this happen. The mind isn't concerned with how we feel about something, but it does have thoughts and opinions *about* it. The mind will give us advice on what makes sense, but it's the heart that tells us how we feel about it.

The mind is our assistant to bring what we desire into form. Desire comes first and from the heart . . . we *want* something. With the mind's help, we then make plans as to how to make that happen in form. Finally we take the action that both feels good and makes sense, to achieve our desire in the best possible way. This is the heart and mind in sync and in balance, or whole-heartedness.

Great minds have invented many amazing things, but the idea or inspiration for those things came through the heart. When the heart and mind are in sync, the flow of energy is unimpeded, the cycle continues to flow and all the rooms of our life feel great to us. This is the optimal cycle of life that brings us happiness and fulfillment and helps us thrive.

# The Rooms According to Feng Shui

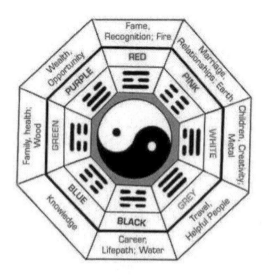

*Feng Shui: (In Chinese thought) a system of laws considered to govern spatial arrangement and orientation in relation to the flow of energy (qi), and whose favorable or unfavorable effects are taken into account when siting and designing buildings.*

The picture on the preceding page is the classic feng shui Bagua (pronounced bah gua), which is in the shape of an octagon, a shape that's considered good energy in feng shui. I placed it here at the beginning to give you an idea of the nine rooms as seen through the eyes of a feng shui consultant. Don't worry, I'll simplify this as we proceed!

Feng shui is an ancient Chinese art that focuses on *placement and balance*. It teaches that what you create in your spaces is a reflection of your inner way of being, just as what is going on inside your head shows up in your living/working spaces. It teaches that your physical spaces reflect your desires, talents and beliefs about your world and who you are. If you're having challenges in some area of your life, these challenges will show up as an imbalance or stuck energy in your spaces. When someone is able to see their spaces as a reflection or mirror of their life, they are able to see their life from a new perspective, one they've created in their spaces. As they shift their spaces to feel better, their life naturally begins to feel better. When you have a more conscious awareness of how imbalances in your life show up in your spaces, you see them from a more powerful perspective to make changes in your life, and you form
a deeper relationship with them as well. This empowers you to have more control over your life.

## Living a Balanced Life

Feng shui is a technique that helps bring a space—and therefore someone's life—into *balance*. Balance is the state of being where all power and strength lie. As an analogy, when you stand squarely on your feet and are grounded and centered, you are a powerfully strong force and someone would have a hard time pushing you off that center. But if you lean even slightly to either side—when you get *out of balance*—a person can easily knock you off your stance.

This is the analogy of your life. When energy is flowing in all areas and is in balance, you have lots of energy, you have good awareness and power to live a full life. Going back to the first part of this book, when you live well in every room or part of your life, you live what is referred to as *a balanced life.*

## Balance is Best

Feng shui is all about balance. Energy sometimes gets stuck or blocked and needs a little push to get it flowing again, and sometimes it needs a shove to get it moving and bring the space into balance. An imbalance is simply energy that isn't flowing freely and optimally. We intuitively know when something is out of balance — *it just doesn't feel good.* I may suggest several things to do, but usually one suggestion will feel best to a client.

As in the rooms of your life, the feng shui cycle begins in the Center and then flows outward into the Life Path gua and continues around the wheel of life in a clockwise direction through the other eight *guas.*

The basic idea in feng shui is that you will generally live a healthy and harmonious life if your spaces reflect your inner balance, and vice versa—because one is a mirror of the other. If the energy is allowed to flow freely into and through each room of your physical spaces, you'll have an easier time getting through life challenges.

Your home should be your sanctuary, the one place where you can rest, rejuvenate and replenish your energy to face another day. If it's unused or allowed to get cluttered, or it just doesn't feel good when you walk in the door, your home zaps your energy more than replenishes it, so you're unable to deal optimally with the challenges that come your way.

If the energy gets stagnant or stuck in one part of your life, it slows down available energy to the other parts. You'll understand this if you're familiar with the term "workaholic," which describes people who spend most of their time and energy at a job or career, causing the rest of their life to suffer from the inattention. In feng shui, this workaholic imbalance shows up in the Success gua and may be seen as clutter or disorganization.

Our bodies are our vehicles to move us around on the planet, and they are built to be healthy and in balance throughout our time here. However, because of genetics, lifestyle and all the chemicals we're exposed to in foods and in our environment, rarely does one sustain a level of excellent health for long. Any illness or dis-ease on any level is an imbalance which begins as pure thought, pure energy. This is the best time to catch the imbalance and shift it. You do this by looking at what's *off* in your life. It's a lot easier to shift it when it's still an energetic imbalance than when it becomes physical.

## What is Stuck Energy?

In the tradition of feng shui, your personal energy, as well as the energy of your spaces, is meant to flow. If it doesn't, you'll feel *off balance* in some way. For example, you may walk into a room and think, "something just doesn't feel right." There may be a room you don't like to go into but not know why.

There are all kinds of ways that energy gets stuck in your life, and your barometer to tell you this is how you *feel*. Your spaces may *look* fine, but something just doesn't feel right. This means some part of your life is out of whack—because in feng shui, it's always reflected in your spaces.

Stuck energy can also show up as something physical, such as poorly placed or crowded furniture, poor light, messiness, or clutter. I've given talks about the value of clutter because it's such an in-your-face reflection of stuck energy. Clutter literally stops energy flow. If you have clutter in a room that's located in your Opportunity and Wealth gua, you'll most likely have challenges finding ways to move forward in your life, and you may also have abundance issues (finances or feeling poorly) unless you shift the energy of that space by clearing the clutter. If you ignore it completely, you may eventually experience imbalances in the areas of your life following that gua. The stuck energy in one gua naturally hinders or impedes energy flow into the succeeding guas on the cycle. So, if you have clutter, it's a really good idea to deal with it!

# The Rooms of the Bagua

| Opportunity<br>Wealth | Success<br>Fame | Relationship<br>Marriage |
|---|---|---|
| Family<br>Ancestry | Balance<br>Health | Creativity<br>Children |
| Knowledge<br>Self | Life Path<br>Career | Helpful People<br>Travel |

*I used to live in a room full of mirrors; all I could see was me. I take my spirit and I crash my mirrors, now the whole world is here for me to see.*

*- Jimmy Hendrix*

This is a very simplified illustration of the Bagua. It shows the nine rooms that make up your life as it relates to your spaces, from the perspective of feng shui.

The Bagua is used to show that our spaces are a reflection of our lives. If there is an imbalance in one part of a space, the Bagua will show how that blockage can reflect a blockage in that particular area of someone's life. In effect, your life shows up in your spaces—and your spaces will reflect how you're doing in your life. I'll explain how that works, from this feng shui perspective.

When you look at this picture of the Bagua, you'll see there are nine squares. Each square is called a *gua* and together, all nine make up the whole Bagua. Each gua represents a physical space that reflects a particular part of someone's life.

In the first part of this book I referred to the various parts of your life as rooms. Here, I am using the term *rooms* to refer to the *physical spaces* that reflect a particular part of your life, because this is the feng shui perspective.

As I mentioned previously, I believe there is a lot of value in using feng shui wisdom to discuss the whole of someone's life. You may notice that the names of the rooms are slightly different, because these are what they're called in the feng shui tradition. However, the purpose, aspect and energy of the rooms are the same.

The word *space* here means any physical area you spend time in. This is typically your home, which can be a 15,000-square-foot mansion or a 300-square-foot trailer. It includes other spaces as well, such as a commercial building, an office, or even your car. The Bagua can be used as a template that represents the floorplan of a whole living space, such as the floorplan of a home or business, or it can be a template for the floorplan of one room. It can also be used for a lot or piece of land. I've discovered that there are many layers to using feng shui, and it took me weeks to learn how to use the Bagua, so don't let it intimidate you!

As a feng shui consultant, I typically begin the inside tour of a home or business at the front door. The Bagua is oriented with the front door at the bottom of the diagram, so it's usually located on one of the bottom squares of the Bagua. When you stand at the front door looking inside, you'll be entering into one of the three bottom guas: Knowledge on the left, Life Path in the middle or Helpful People on the right. Because the front door of a home is usually located in the front and middle of the structure, this typically puts it in the Life Path gua.

Now that you've got the Bagua placement in the proper position, you can see the location of the guas or nine rooms, with Opportunity in the back left and Relationship in the back right of the floorplan. This gives you a general idea of how the Bagua is used as a tool for your physical spaces.

Many people get confused about how to orient the Bagua onto their spaces, because the floorplan of a house or space is rarely square like this picture. The Bagua is only this shape on paper because it's easy to see the nine areas, but this gives you a basic idea of where they are on the floorplan of any space. I won't go into detail about this because it's something that needs a lot more explanation beyond the scope of this discussion—and isn't necessary for the purpose of this book. I've included it to give you a general idea of how rooms and spaces reflect parts of your life.

I receive requests for feng shui assistance for all sorts of reasons: someone is having trouble maintaining or getting over a relationship, feeling stuck in a job, dealing with family issues, or simply thinking "my life just doesn't feel right anymore." Let's say, for instance, a parent is dealing with a rebellious or troubled child. I know there will probably be some kind of energy imbalance in the Family and Ancestry area of their space and most likely an imbalance in the child's room as well. Someone recovering from a bad divorce and having trouble moving into a new life will have some kind of stuck energy in the Relationship gua of their space, and there may be something to look at in their bedroom. As feng shui teaches, a problem or issue in some part of your life shows up as an energy imbalance in that particular area or gua of your space. I've seen this to be true in all my consultations.

I believe I can sense these imbalances, not only because I've been trained to do so, but because I've never been in that space before. I bring what I call *fresh eyes* to it and can see and sense things that someone who's been living in that space day after day has become used to and doesn't really *see* anymore. This is *the elephant in the room* theory. A visitor says, "what's that elephant doing in your living room?" And you say, "what elephant?" A feng shui consultant is trained to not only see the elephant in the living room but also to help it on its way out of your life.

As a feng shui consultant, I make suggestions based on what I feel will help shift the energy, but I never tell a client they *must* do something. It's my client's space and it's their decision to do what feels best to them. I speak what I see and feel and offer ways to shift the energy to get it in balance and flowing again, but it's my client's work to take note of my suggestions and then do what they feel is the best for them, because they live there.

As I go into a detailed explanation of each gua or room I'll mention various physical things that can help get or keep the energy flowing, such as a piece of furniture or art that fits well in that area. These are suggestions to give you a general idea of things that help shift energy. I've found that many people are very intuitive about where they place something or the use of color in a particular gua. Remember, in feng shui it's all about balance, and when an area is in balance, it naturally feels good.

If your spaces feel good right now, congratulations! Your spaces as well as your life are in balance. If there are areas that don't feel good, the following suggestions may help.

Because this is a slightly different way to look at the cycle of life, one based on your spaces in the feng shui tradition, we begin a tour of this map by entering through the front door. Here I will assume that means we enter into the Life Path gua.

# Life Path or Career

| | | |
|---|---|---|
| Opportunity<br>Wealth | Success<br>Fame | Relationship<br>Marriage |
| Family<br>Ancestry | Balance<br>Health | Creativity<br>Children |
| Knowledge<br>Self | Life Path<br>Career | Helpful People<br>Travel |

*I think our life is a journey, and we make mistakes, and it's how we learn from these mistakes and rebound from them that sets us on the path that we're meant to be on.*

- Jay Ellis

*Surfing is a life path. You have to really commit. You have to let go and have faith that it's gonna work out when you take off.*

- Peter Heller

In feng shui, this Life Path gua is also known as the Career gua. This isn't your job, however, it's your *life career*, it's the lessons you came here to learn. The gua related to your job comes later.

Anyone who visits you for the first time begins to get an idea of who you are, as they park in the driveway and walk to the front door. First impressions about who lives here begin outside. Is the landscaping lush and neatly trimmed or is it wild and free? Are there children's toys scattered around, is there an old rusty car in the driveway? Is the house visible from the road or is it tucked behind trees? Does the structure look well maintained or neglected? These impressions are received either consciously or subconsciously, but the visitors are forming an impression about the kind of person or people who live here.

This gua is where the front door is typically located, and where first-time visitors usually enter your home. Those who live here may walk in from the garage or a side door, but the front door is considered to be the main point of entry.

The front door is known as the *mouth* of the house, because it says a lot about who lives inside. Are there cobwebs around it, are the windows on the door clean and free of cracks? If there a doormat to wipe feet or is the one there too small and unassuming? Because guests and visitors usually enter through the front door, they get an initial impression of what kind of person or family lives here. Does the entrance feel welcoming and warm, or is it dark and closed in? Either way, it says something about who lives inside. It's called an entrance because it's meant to *entrance* people when they walk in. What do visitors see—and feel—when they first enter your space?

## Feng Shui Aspects of the Life Path Gua

<u>Energy</u>
*Water* is the energy represented in this gua, because it's the analogy of your birth out of the water of the womb as a human being to begin your Life Path.

<u>Colors</u>
Indigo and deep blues, because they represent deep water.

<u>Shapes</u>
Wavy patterns, like waves of water.

<u>Placement of Forms</u>
Anything that has a wavy pattern and/or is deep blue. A water fountain, one with the water flowing up and out. Pictures/paintings of pastoral water scenes—not storms, however, because you don't want to bring in the energy of a *stormy* life!

## Example

A designer friend of mine bought an old house for her business, and she asked me to feng shui it before she moved in, to help make her business successful. We began in the foyer, in the Life Path/Career gua.

When I walked through the front door, directly ahead was a 20-foot hallway that ended into a kitchen with windows that looked out on the back yard. There were several doors and doorways off this long hallway, leading to offices and storage areas. Directly to the right and left of the entrance were doors leading to what would become her office and a conference room.

I explained that this area is related to her life path/career. In this case, we worked with the energy of this space to help her business, which she also felt was her life's work. There was no energy held in this small foyer (this gua) because it was shooting down the hall and scattered around by all those doorways.

The foyer is the prelude into the space; it's meant to *entrance* guests when they walk in, to hold their attention (energy) for a bit before they look around. The long hallway directed their attention (carried their energy) all the way out to the back yard, and the doorways were also elements of distraction (scattered energy). I told her she needed to make this area so enticing, so interesting, that people would walk in and just look around here for a bit, not all over the house right away. She took my suggestions and did beautiful things with them!

I was invited back for her Open House and got to see and feel the results of her work. I walked in the front door and immediately looked down at the beautiful rug she placed there, it was very eye (and energy) catching! She'd put a creative *water wall* fountain to the left of the front door, another eye/energy-catcher, and had painted this area a bright cerulean blue, very sumptuous. After I looked at all this, I then noticed her office and the hallway, the walls now hung with design drawings and examples of her work. I got to experience the sense of my own energy doing exactly what I'd intended when making those suggestions to her. She'd taken my other suggestions for the rest of her space, and it all looked and felt great. Needless to say, her business thrived.

# Knowledge of Self

| Opportunity<br>Wealth | Success<br>Fame | Relationship<br>Marriage |
|---|---|---|
| Family<br>Ancestry | Balance<br>Health | Creativity<br>Children |
| Knowledge<br>Self | Life Path<br>Career | Helpful People<br>Travel |

*Self-knowledge is no guarantee of happiness, but it is on the side of happiness and can supply the courage to fight for it.*

- Simone de Beauvoir

*I actually think there's an incredible amount of self-knowledge that comes with getting older.*

- Jamie Lee Curtis

You've come out of the deep waters of the womb and have embarked on your life path. You now look out at the world around you and find ways to discover who you are. In the cycle of a whole life, this area could be seen as the toddler phase, a time of curiosity and self-discovery, a deep desire to know who you are and how you can live your purpose. You gain knowledge about yourself, your world and how you want to make your way in it. The energy is similar to the room of Knowledge written about previously.

This gua is the left front of your space, as you enter the front door. Because this room represents knowledge of self and the world, it feels good to place things here that represent and reflect this. It's a great place for meditation and journaling or planning your next adventure.

## Feng Shui Aspects of the Knowledge Gua

Energy
Because you're growing into more of who you are, this gua holds the energy of *wood*, like the trunk of a tree expanding up and out.

Colors
Lighter blues, aqua and blue-greens. You're coming out of the watery depths and growing as you put your feet on the earth.

Shapes
Columnar, like the trunk of a tree, columns on a porch or even vertical-striped wallpaper.

Placement of Forms

Put a special chair in here, one you love to sit in to journal and meditate. Live plants or anything that grows are good—but if you can't keep them alive, substitute silk plants and flowers instead.

A word about dried flowers: because these were alive at one time but are not now, they're considered *dead energy* and are not "good feng shui" for your spaces. Some would say the same is true of cut flowers, but let your intuition be your guide here. Certainly, throw them out once they begin to wilt.

# Example

Using myself as an example, I owned a house with a den in this gua that I used as my home office. I placed a comfy upholstered chair with an ottoman here and sat in it to journal, meditate and read inspirational books. I journaled every day and it always felt very good to me, sitting in that room. Guests called this "Val's room" because they sensed so much of my energy in here. I still try to place that chair in the Knowledge area wherever I live.

# Family and Ancestry

| Opportunity<br>Wealth | Success<br>Fame | Relationship<br>Marriage |
|---|---|---|
| Family<br>Ancestry | Balance<br>Health | Creativity<br>Children |
| Knowledge<br>Self | Life Path<br>Career | Helpful People<br>Travel |

*Families are like branches on a tree. We grow in different directions, yet our roots remain as one.*

- from *Good Housekeeping* magazine

*Every man is a quotation from all his ancestors.*

- Ralph Waldo Emerson

Even though this gua, like all the other guas, will be relevant in different ways throughout your whole life, this one could be thought of as the *teen* phase of life. You're pushing the boundaries to know yourself on a deeper level as you learn more about your immediate family and those who came before you.

The energy of this gua is the same as the room of Family discussed earlier in this book, with its purpose in learning about our family, culture and ancestry when we're young and being the elder of that family when we reach the age of wisdom. The term *family* takes on different meanings, and often becomes more meaningful to us, as we spiral back around to it at various points in our life.

## Feng Shui Aspects of the Family Gua

### Energy

Because you are still growing, the energy is still *wood*. You are now more aware of not only the branches on the tree but are also becoming aware of your family roots, and that you're an integral part of this whole tree.

### Colors

Greens, from deep evergreen to soft shades of green.

### Shapes

Again, it's about growth, so anything columnar. Plants and flowers, alive or silk, and paintings of nature scenes.

Placement of Forms

Put things here that represent your family, ancestry or culture. This is a great place to hang family photos or have family albums here. If you do genealogy and have a representation of your family tree, this is a wonderful place to hang it.

# Example

I did a consult with a woman who was part Cherokee Indian. She owned a beautiful feathered headdress that she had enclosed in glass and hung in this area. She wanted to honor her ancestry by displaying this headdress and gave it a place of honor. It was a beautiful and powerful way to show her ancestry, and she intuitively hung it in the best possible place, even though she knew almost nothing about feng shui.

# Opportunity and Wealth

| Opportunity Wealth | Success Fame | Relationship Marriage |
|---|---|---|
| Family Ancestry | Balance Health | Creativity Children |
| Knowledge Self | Life Path Career | Helpful People Travel |

*If opportunity doesn't knock, build a door.*

– Milton Berle

*If a window of opportunity opens, don't pull down the shade.*

*- Tom Peters*

You now move out into the world and seek opportunities that will help you be successful in your life. As discussed earlier in the room of Opportunity, this could mean further education, getting a job doing something you enjoy, embarking upon a career or even traveling to different parts of the world to experience other cultures. Opportunities can come in all sorts of shapes and sizes and from many different directions, so it's important to feel *anticipation* rather than expectation.

In feng shui, this gua is also known as the Wealth gua, because it's here you gather the funds needed to make opportunities successful. Wealth is usually related to how much money one has, but true wealth is more about the energy of *abundance*. The inside feeling of being able to live in the richness of life opens up new opportunities that money can't buy. You might also think about the *wealth of opportunities* available to you at any one point.

Money is a physical measure of wealth, but the *energy* of wealth is abundance, meaning it's more important how you *feel about* what you have than the actual thing itself. Money is an opportunistic tool in many ways, but money itself can become an excuse, blaming the lack of money for missed opportunities, when in truth it's how one holds the thoughts and beliefs about money and abundance that can be the root of money issues.

# Feng Shui Aspects of the Opportunity Gua

Energy
Because you're in the world, seeking new opportunities and experiences, the energy here is *wind,* so it's important to keep the energy flowing, moving like the wind.

Shapes
There is no shape in this gua, as wind is pure energy.

Colors
Hues of purple. Purple is considered to be a spiritual color and represents the mystery of inspirational ideas for opportunities that come from the desires of our heart.

Placement of Forms
Hanging a wind chime in this area is a classic feng shui enhancement, because it's designed to chime in the wind. Hang it with the intention that opportunities are wafting their way to you! Also, placing dragonflies, hummingbirds, or other flying beings are good representations of things that move in the wind.

# Example

A man asked me for help in finding a fulfilling job, one that he would enjoy and want to stay with for years. He'd had a few jobs in the past, but nothing he really liked. The economy was tight and he was having trouble finding something that felt good. His house was clean and neat, and his sister/decorator helped him with color and placement, so as we walked around his home, the energy felt fine.

We came to a guest bedroom in this gua. The door was closed. I explained that this room represents the opportunities he's looking for, so let's take a look. He said, "do we have to?" and I knew then this was where his energy was stuck. He opened the door, walked in and tears came into his eyes. The room looked like a tornado had gone through it. It was dark, blinds drawn, curtain rod sagged and crooked. The bed and dresser were piled high with stuff. It was very unlike the rest of his space. The energy was stuck here, a clear indication of why he was having trouble finding a job.

I asked him to tell me about this room. He said his father had become very sick and could no longer function on his own, so he moved him in here. His dad didn't die in this room, but he died on the way to the hospital about six months ago, and now he just couldn't stand to be in this room because it brought up too many painful memories.

I explained that the flow of energy was stuck in this room. Being the Opportunity gua, it was preventing him from getting a job. He understood but wondered how he could clear it when he couldn't even step into the room. I suggested he have a family member or a good friend help him or hire a professional. It was important to clear this room and get the energy moving again. If he didn't, not only would he continue to have challenges finding a suitable job but it could affect the gua next to it, Success, and he probably wouldn't be successful in any job he did find.

I heard from him about three months later. He said his sister and brother helped him clear the room and they'd actually had some laughs thinking of memories with their dad. Not only did he find a job, but it was one with great career potential and he knew he was going to love being part of the team.

# Success and Fame

| | | |
|---|---|---|
| Opportunity<br>Wealth | Success<br>Fame | Relationship<br>Marriage |
| Family<br>Ancestry | Balance<br>Health | Creativity<br>Children |
| Knowledge<br>Self | Life Path<br>Career | Helpful People<br>Travel |

*The secret of success is to be ready when your opportunity comes.*

– Benjamin Disraeli

*For success, attitude is as important as ability.*

- Walter Scott

Congratulations, you've become a success in your life! This is the area where you honor that achievement, whatever it means to you.

As it relates to feng shui, *success* is the realization of what you set out to do when you were born. It's also called the Fame gua, because you may be a good example of how to achieve success and people may look up to you. You've become known by others as one who has achieved their desires and has *made it* in life, in some way. Again, this doesn't necessarily mean a job or career, it can be any goal you've worked toward where others have followed your progress and now see you as successful. In this way you now are *famous* for your achievements and can be a real-life example of personal success to other people in your life.

## Feng Shui Aspects of the Success Gua

Energy
Because you're now ready to express yourself with what you've achieved, the energy here is *fire*. . .you're *on fire* with life.

Shapes
Anything that represents fire, similar to tongues of flame moving up and/or out. Candles are considered the icon of fire energy because they hold fire. Cactus and succulent plants, because of their needles, star shapes or things that sparkle also represent fire.

## Colors

Any shades of red or orange that are pleasing to you, that *light you up.*

## Placement of Forms

Candles of any shape or color are good in this area, because they hold actual fire. Degrees, diplomas or certificates hung on the walls are great examples of success. Place things here that make you *feel successful* when you look at them—it may be photos of your children or a house you helped build.

A fireplace in this area is great if you have one here. But no matter where a fireplace is located in your spaces, make sure *fire* is represented in it in some way, because that is the purpose of this *fire-place.* Light fires in the winter and place candles in or on the hearth in the warmer months. Used with the intention of increasing energy in a space, candles are good to *light it up.* In this gua they're used to honor the energy of success—because here you are on fire in the expression of your successful life!

## Example

I did a consult for a woman who wanted help selling her condo. The kitchen was in this gua. It was all white—cabinets, countertops and appliances and tile floor. I explained that it would be good to put some red and/or fire touches here, like hand towels, a rug in front of the sink, maybe a red teapot, some red candles, etc.

I got a call from her about a month later and she told me an interesting story. She was hosting an open house for her neighbors and friends to let them know about the sale. She'd done everything I suggested for the kitchen—purchased red rugs, red towels, a red teapot and a few candles. She lit the candles and went into another room to grab her phone. When she went back into the kitchen, a towel she'd placed on the counter was too close to a burner and started to catch fire! Luckily, she caught it in plenty of time and there was no problem. She asked me if maybe she'd overdone the "fire thing" with too much red. I laughed and said she was right about that! Feng shui is about balance, and she'd obviously over-balanced the fire energy! Thank goodness it was a lesson learned without mishap.

Another client was a hairdresser who wanted to increase her business, but she'd become discouraged because it wasn't happening. She didn't have any idea what it would take to spiff up her salon and then summon the energy to do the networking necessary to get more clients, so she asked for help.

Her salon was in the back part of an old building and there was a fireplace in this gua. It was old and dark and she didn't even know if the chimney was stable enough to have a fire. I explained that a fireplace is created to be a "place for fire" and it needed to have more energy, especially with it being in this particular gua of her business. We talked about doing several things with the fireplace, from having a chimney sweep come out and give her a report, to tearing it down altogether. I also suggested spiffing up the fireplace itself, making it a fun focal point for her clients while they waited.

She ended up getting a report from a sweep, who told her a real fire would be too intense, but she could use manufactured fire logs in it. She painted the brick a soft gray and had a beautiful natural-wood mantle made for it. She bought a fun screen and put candles in and around it. Then she hung a mobile made of brightly colored stars to hang on one side. A trio of comfortable chairs and a small coffee table with interesting magazines made up the cozy scenario. Her clients loved it and told their friends about the beautiful salon. This not only brought in more business, but it gave her more energy to go out and do the networking that did indeed bring her more business!

# Relationship and Marriage

| Opportunity Wealth | Success Fame | Relationship Marriage |
|---|---|---|
| Family Ancestry | Balance Health | Creativity Children |
| Knowledge Self | Life Path Career | Helpful People Travel |

*Everything is expressed through relationship. Colour can exist only through other colours, dimension through other dimensions, position through other positions that oppose them.*

- Piet Mondrian

*Treasure your relationships, not your possessions.*

- Anthony J. D'Angelo

Now that you're so successful in your life, you become interested in developing intimate relationships with significant others in your life. This can be a marriage or partnership, but the energy is all about love, and it also includes more than *being in love*. On the highest level of living in and with love, it's ultimately about the love relationship you have with yourself—and this can be the most challenging one of all!

As discussed earlier in this book, relationships come in all shapes and sizes and in all kinds of ways. In this gua, you honor these significant relationships. This room is different from that of the family and ancestry gua, as it relates to the *choices* you make when you meet and fall in love with someone, a very different love than the love you feel for your family.

You've been on fire, moving out into the world to express yourself in some way, and now it feels good to ground your energy with personal relationships.

This gua is also about a relationship with the energy that is earth; some call this Gaia. Here, you get a deeper understanding of what it means to be a human on this amazingly beautiful planet, sharing your energy with it.

## Feng Shui Aspects of the Relationship Gua

### Energy

The ground of *Earth*, representing your physical connection to the energy of the earth, which some call Gaia. You now become aware of the relationship you have with Nature as you walk on the earth and receive its deep healing energies. Earth was created to be our human playground, and because we are *grounded* to it, we have a visceral and deep connection with it.

Color
Earth tones, from brown to rust, and also pink tones. Pink is considered to be the color of the energy of love. Have you heard of sending someone a *pink fuzzy*? This is consciously sending them the wonderful energy of love.

Shape
Square or rectangular, which represents being *grounded* and having a solid foundation on the Earth.

Placement
Because this gua is about *relationship*, it's important to have pairs of things here—two chairs, two lamps, two pillows, two pictures. If you want to be in a relationship, place something that represents your ideal relationship in this area. The Yin-Yang symbol is the icon of relationship.

# Example

A woman was ready to have a partner in her life again and asked me to feng shui her space to increase her chances of a man showing up in her life. She'd been divorced for five years and was ready for another relationship. Her bedroom was in this gua, and I noticed that she had lots of family photos, but none that represented the kind of relationship she was looking for. There was one chair, two nightstands but only one with a lamp on it.

After explaining about placing pairs of things here, I suggested she get another lamp and put the chair in another room or find another one similar to it. She had a few icons of *pairs* in other areas of her home—a painting of two lovebirds and a yin-yang symbol that she could place in this area. I also suggested she do a *vision board* as a way to picture the qualities of the man she desired to be with now. It's simple to do: find magazine photos of happy couples doing fun things together, along with words and pictures that represent what's wanted in a relationship, and paste them in a collage fashion on poster paper. She should then place this vision board somewhere in the room where she could see it often, or even under her mattress . . . so she could *sleep on it.*

*Note: a vision board is like a visual template that holds the vision or idea of what you desire. You can do this exercise for just about anything you want to have, be or do.*

I also noticed an outbuilding in her back yard, but there was no path to it from the house. Using the Bagua as a reference for her whole property, this storage shed was located in the back right or Relationship gua of her lot. Because there was no path to this shed, she was *disconnected* from the energy of relationship. I suggested that she consider making some kind of path to it, which would connect it to the relationship gua in her home.

She groaned when I told her this, saying her ex-husband loved that shed. He'd go out there to smoke cigars and hang out with his buddies, so she had no desire to do anything with it. I told her if she wanted a new relationship now, she needed to shift the energy in that shed to make it her own and then connect it with her house, to honor her new intention.

We discussed several options to make a path and she chose the one that was doable for her and felt the best. I saw her at a networking function a few months later and she told me about the new man in her life!

# Creativity and Children

| Opportunity Wealth | Success Fame | Relationship Marriage |
|---|---|---|
| Family Ancestry | Balance Health | Creativity Children |
| Knowledge Self | Life Path Career | Helpful People Travel |

*Make an empty space in any corner of your mind, and creativity will instantly fill it.*

- Dee Hock

*Creativity is a natural extension of our enthusiasm.*

- Earl Nightingale

Creativity is our personal and unique expression in form that comes naturally as a result of our life experiences. Think about how you *feel* when you look at a work of art. You are tapping into how this person felt about what was happening in their life at a certain point. This drove him or her to express their emotions in this particular way.

The urge to be creative is innately within us from birth. Many choose to creatively express this urge as a result of a life-changing experience. Some simply express the gift of love and gratitude for a life well lived. No matter how it is expressed, this is the area where you let your "inner child" out to play!

This gua includes children, because a child is the ultimate creative expression resulting from the relationship between sperm and egg. It's a creation we really have nothing to do with. We simply put the *seeds* in the right place and then leave it up Godness to decide if it wants to grow a body or not. We are all mysteriously made from a creative life force energy and so are gifted with the desire to use this energy to be creative.

Being creative is a natural desire in human beings, and like any desire, there's a longing to express it in some way. It begins in childhood and continues through life. Children don't have the critical mind yet, so they create without judgment or fear. But as we age, we hear criticism either from others or in our own mind.

Fear is a big stumbling block to creativity, and even the most famous artists will confess they sometimes have to push past their fears of "I'm not good enough" to offer their creations to the world. This gua is not about becoming an artist, but it *is* about expressing that creative urge in some way.

We feel the desire to create something because it's an innate part of who we are, but our minds can get in the way and tell us who we are *not*, effectively pouring water on that inner fire. The truth is, expressing this creative urge in some way is an important, and even necessary, part of living a balanced life. Stifling it cuts off a large part of our connection to the totality of who we are. Nature expresses this creative desire automatically and on a continuous basis—partly because it doesn't have a mind to sabotage it!

Push past any fears or doubts and simply make or do something that feels fun, silly, happy, simple or complex. Your inner child is waiting for you to help it have fun! You don't have to show what you did to anyone, and you can forget about it or throw it away when you're done. The point is to just begin . . .

## Feng Shui Aspects of the Creativity Gua

Energy
*Metal.* You've grounded yourself in the Relationship gua and now you're digging into the ground, into the heart of your desire, to discover treasures with which to create something that represents the depth of who you've become.

Shapes
Circular or oval.

Colors
White, like a blank canvas. White represents the ultimate creative potential because it holds the energy of all colors. Because it's also represented by unearthed treasures, colors are any metal or gem tones that come out of the ground—gold, silver, ruby, jade, etc.

Placement of Forms
Any objects that are circular or oval, like pillows, trays or tables. If you're an artist, this is a great place for your tools. An artist's studio would fit well here. This is the place for your inner child so place things here that feel happy, fun and whimsical.

## Example

A client lived in a house with a laundry room in this gua. It was spacious, lots of cabinets and counter space. One wall was empty, with nothing on it. A child's desk sat along this wall. My client said her daughter liked to sit here and play while she was doing laundry. I saw the blank wall as a perfect *canvas* upon which to be creative and suggested she paint it with chalk paint. Her daughter could then draw all kinds of things on the wall, wipe it off and begin again. The mother thought this was a great idea and said she'd love to doodle right along with her daughter. It was a perfect way to play with her daughter and her own inner child, and honor this gua of creativity.

In my own space in my Creativity gua, I've hung several sketches of *Story People* by Brian Andreas. Every time I look at them I smile, in appreciation for Mr. Andreas' inner-child creativity and his ability to say very meaningful things in such simple, whimsical ways.

# Helpful People and Travel

| | | |
|---|---|---|
| Opportunity<br>Wealth | Success<br>Fame | Relationship<br>Marriage |
| Family<br>Ancestry | Balance<br>Health | Creativity<br>Children |
| Knowledge<br>Self | Life Path<br>Career | Helpful People<br>Travel |

*I wanted to support things that are helpful to people and maybe bash what I think is dangerous. So I switched from being everybody to being myself.*

- Jenny Holzer

*People are so helpful. People will stop what they're doing to show you something, to walk with you through a section of the town, or explain how a suspension bridge really works.*

- David McCullough

This is the part of your life in which you take your whole self, the culmination of a life well lived, the creative self that has experienced so much in life and offer it to the world as a *helpful person*. It now starts to feel important to give back in some way, to share some of the gifts of wisdom you've received throughout your life.

Being a helpful person shows up in all kinds of ways. It may be that you volunteer a few hours a month or sit for the grandkids while their parents are at work. You may spend a few hours as a bagger at a grocery store just because you want the interaction with people. Or you may become an activist, championing for the rights of others or the world. No matter what you do, this gua is about offering the wisdom of your whole self to others.

This is also known as the Travel gua because you may travel out into the larger world and interact with people outside your immediate sphere. You may travel to group functions or companies where you're a vital elder member on the board, or travel to another country to help those in need.

In feng shui, with the view of life as a cycle from birth to death, this gua is the last one before the return Home to the Center or source from which you were created. It's the time where you take stock of your life and begin to consider the value of sharing what you've come to know. This is a time when many people make what's called their *Bucket List* of things they want to do before they leave. A hilarious movie about this is called *The Bucket List*, with Jack Nicholson and Morgan Freeman.

## Feng Shui Aspects of the Helpful People Gua

Energy
Again, this is *metal*. You're offering the depths of who you are to the world. This is represented by any metal, stone or gem that comes out of the earth.

Shape
Circular or oval.

Color
Gray or silver, gold and any gem tones.

Placement of Forms
Place any icons of achievement here, such as awards or letters of recognition, even something that represents a challenge that you've overcome. These are beyond the diplomas of education or work that feel better in the Success gua. These represent achievements of a life well lived. If you've learned to play the guitar and go to local pubs to play, this gua is the best place for your guitar. Place the book you've written in this area as a symbol of achievement in helping others through your writing. This area is where you place a symbol or an expression of—or your desire to be—a helpful person in some way.

# Example

The owner/broker of a local real estate company asked me to help shift the energy of the building she owned and used for her business. Her business was expanding so she'd hired more staff and needed more office space. The location was desirable so she didn't want to move, but the building needed some major updating. Because the property had room for expansion, she hired a contractor to design and build additional space.

Her own office was currently located in the back left of the building, in the Opportunity gua, which had worked out well because she'd taken advantage of several opportunities and her company was growing, and she'd become successful in her industry. I suggested that she move her office into the Helpful People gua. She'd been in the business many years and had accumulated a lot of experience (and wisdom) about the real estate industry. As such, she was very wise and savvy—the ultimate *helpful person* to mentor her staff on their own journey to success. She was delighted with this suggestion and had the blueprints redrawn to place her office here.

# Balance and Health

| | | |
|---|---|---|
| Opportunity<br>Wealth | Success<br>Fame | Relationship<br>Marriage |
| Family<br>Ancestry | Balance<br>Health | Creativity<br>Children |
| Knowledge<br>Self | Life Path<br>Career | Helpful People<br>Travel |

*Life is like riding a bicycle . . . to keep your balance you must keep moving.*

- Albert Einstein

*The essence of health is inner balance.*

- Andrew Weil

In the first part of this book, this gua is the room called Center, because it represents the source from which life springs, which is also true here. In feng shui, it's called the Balance and Health gua because it's the source energy around which the cycle of a life spins. This area needs to be *in balance* to maintain the health and well-being of someone's life. On a floor plan, this gua is the middle or center of a space.

Because this is the center of a space, it's represented as the center of those who live within it. Just as the sun radiates its energy out equally from its center to light everything around it, the energy of the Balance and Health gua radiates out into each of the other guas. The influence of its energy radiates out to affect the whole space, and therefore affects the balance, functioning and flow of all the other guas in that space. Being that the space reflects the lives of those who live within it, the balance, functioning and flow of their whole lives are affected as well. If this gua is out of balance or ignored for any length of time, our lives get out of balance, which can affect our health on the mental or even physical level.

In a residence, the middle of a floor plan often has a hallway, stairway, half bath, closets, or pantry and is a passageway between the front and back, so it may be a challenge to think of how to maintain balance here. Because it can be such a multi-functional space, it's even more important to maintain a sense of balance here. This is where imagination and creativity come in handy . . .

# Feng Shui Aspects of the Balance/ Health Gua

## Energy

Godness or connection to our Center. Being human innately puts us off balance because we have bodies that show up as male or female. Then we discover that life itself is a balancing act. So maintaining our connection with Godness helps keep us in balance. Just as the sun is the source that allows life to continue on earth, Source is the energy that helps us maintain that life. Without either of these energy sources, we would not be able to function.

## Color

All hues of yellow and orange.

## Shape

Anything that represents Center, the sun, or balance. The yin-yang symbol is an icon of balance. It's not only a balance of black and white moving together, but there's a white dot in the black and a black dot in the white, relating to the importance of both inner and outer balance.

## Placement of Forms

The yin-yang symbol is appropriate here, if it has meaning for you. Possibly the scales of justice for an office. A religious or spiritual statue or painting, a metallic art piece that looks like the sun, or something that represents a connection to your center, all would feel good here.

# Example

As mentioned, the center of houses are typically confusing spaces for representing the energy of balance here. Many people don't want to paint their walls yellow or orange, and even though these are the best colors for this gua, I'd never say someone *must* paint it, because there are other ways to honor it.

A client of mine lived in a house that had a half bath, closet and pantry, as well as a stairway, in this gua, and he did not like yellow or orange. But he did have some shelf space in a nook under the staircase where he could place icons that pertain to this gua. He was a Buddhist and had pictures and owned a beautiful bust of the Buddha, so he put these on a shelf in the nook. He was now honoring the energy of this gua.

The stairway came down into a den where he spent most of his time, but this room *just didn't feel right* to him. He also had some health issues he'd been trying to shift for some time.

In feng shui, a stairway is typically considered *falling energy*, because it comes down from above. Because the Buddha was now sitting directly under this stairway, I told my client to "put the Buddha to work" to shift the intention of it to rising energy, thus helping to stabilize and *balance* the falling energy of the stairs into his den, which would help the den feel better. Now that he'd shifted this falling energy that could be affecting his health, I suggested he envision/meditate on how great he'll feel with excellent health. He could also write down that feeling on a special paper or even do a vision board and place it under the Buddha. The Buddha statue was now

*working* to shift a lot of energy. Not only was its placement
a way to honor this gua, it was also helping to stabilize the
stair energy *and* manifest his vision for perfect health

# The Bottom Line

We're each given a whole life to live, one day at a time, year after year—many years, if it's part of our script. We transition from childhood to adult to elder, and then we drop the body to move on to other adventures. Every minute we're here is an opportunity to look deeper at what IS and become more aware of this gift of life. Awareness gives us more control, because we can make better-informed decisions.

Because of the diversity in the world, we may have many opportunities to enhance the various *rooms* of our life. This naturally affects all the rooms on the whole cycle of our life, as everything is inter-connected. The balance of our life cycle is affected not only by how well we *furnish* or occupy each room, but also by how well we live in all the rooms.

As I've written previously, everything is energy and energy is neutral . . . it just IS. It's our thoughts *about what is* that makes it good or bad/yes or no/dark or light/up or down. Without the mind to label and judge everything, our days, weeks, months, and years would be very peaceful, accepting life as it IS.

Try paying attention to the thoughts that pop into your head when you're not happy about something. The mind has opinions and thoughts about everything, and sometimes they're not in our best interest.

This neutral way of looking at our life helps us to stay in balance as we move through circumstances that feel challenging. When we can look at a problem and think, *this just is what it is*, we don't get lost in the emotional upheaval about it and so are better prepared to deal with it. Yes, this takes practice—but what's more important than taking control of your own life?

We live life one experience at a time, and it's our perspective that determines the outcome. That perspective is born out of what we *believe* to be true, not always what is actually true. As our beliefs color and filter what we experience, it's important to be aware of our inner self—our beliefs, biases, patterns, habits, and thoughts. Our lives are made up of both challenges we've lived through and adventures we wish had lasted forever—and what we personally take away from them is based on what goes on inside.

This is why the analogy of the rooms—both in our lives, and on the Bagua—is valuable. Our life is like a *house* that's made up of many different rooms and each room is important to maintaining the integrity of the whole structure. When we live well in every room, the house or *whole* of our life feels good, we have a strong foundation from which to be in the outside world and face all the experiences that come our way.

When we are more aware of who we are, what motivates us, and how we perceive what's in front of us, the cycle, or energy, of our life keeps flowing. We feel the richness and vitality of a life well and fully lived. The value of feng shui to see how our life shows up in our spaces helps to give us an outer indication of how well we're doing on the cycle.

One of my spiritual teachers once said, "Earth is one big amusement park, and we're here to take in all the rides." I think that's a good beginning for lightening up and not taking everything so seriously. As the old maxim says, "You'll never get out of this alive"—so why not look for some light in every dark corner?

If you're *in the dark* and unhappy because you see life as something that just happens *to* you, there's a lot of value in learning how to be the candle by becoming *enlightened* about yourself. You can then light your own way to dispel much of the darkness. This is the power of knowing who we are and that we're connected to a source that loves and accepts us right where we are. It's our inner awareness plus this connection that gives us the strength to carry on.

I believe our greatest and most holy task is to see the error in the *thought* that we are separate from Godness. The energy and essence of pure love is not outside of us. It *is* who we really are. It's imperative that we re-turn from the belief that we are separate to claim and own this truth.

Connecting with this energy on an inner level is a great way to begin that return journey. It starts with our desire and willingness to see the purpose and value of living life in a more wholistic way.

I believe that our personal energy affects, and is affected by, everything we think and do and everyone we interact with, so my perspective leans toward life enhancement on the level of energy. I also believe there is value in looking at one's life from the perspective of feng shui, based on the flow of energy in our spaces. I've seen many examples from working with clients that this is a helpful tool to make positive changes in one's life.

I hope that, as a result of reading this book, you've come to more deeply understand and embrace the gift and the power of who you are and the potential you have for thriving in all areas of your life. Go for it—you've got nothing to lose and many good potentials to achieve!

# Recommended Reading and Resources

*The Untethered Soul* by Michael Singer
www.untetheredsoul.com

Several books by Don Miguel Ruiz
www.miguelruiz.com

Several books by Richard Bach
www.richardbach.com

*Loving What Is* by Byron Katie
www.thework.com

*The Power of Now* by Eckhart Tolle
www.eckharttolle.com

*Heal Your Body* by Louise L. Hay
www.hayhouse.com

*A Course in Miracles* by Helen Schucman
www.acim.org

*A Course of Love* by Mari Perron
www.acourseoflove.org

*Wind and Water, Your Personal Feng Shui Journey*
by Carole Hyder
www.windwaterschool.com

*Feng Shui for Dummies* by David Daniel Kennedy
www.dummies.com

*The Five Love Languages* by Gary Chapman
www.5lovelanguages.com

**Book Coaching**:

Maureen Ryan Griffin

mrg@wordplay.com

**Illustrating**:

Ambrea Wright

ambreawright@yahoo.com

# Acknowledgements

The roots of my spiritual perspective on life began in St. Paul, Minnesota, in 1977, with my first spiritual teachers, Bill, Phyllis, and George—angels who flew in from Canada to answer all my questions and helped to *put me on the Path*. They told me I'd never look at the world in the same way again . . . and they were right!

I learned about the Bagua from my creative and wise feng shui teacher, Carol Bridges, who taught the BTB (or "Black Hat") school of feng shui, which is fundamentally based on how spaces feel. I learned much about intuition and following inner guidance while spending time with Carol in her Bryson County, Indiana, school room, a magical place. I'm able to write this book now because I received such a strong and beautiful foundation upon which to grow in awareness of the purpose of my own life and thereby assist others—and now share this knowledge with you in book form.

This book would not be possible without a "download" I received during meditation in the winter of 2018, a piece of wisdom from my connection with my source, what I call Godness. This guidance encouraged me to believe and come to know that I could actually write something of value, that others may benefit from the way I express it. I also want to acknowledge myself for acting upon it. Without my accepting this as truth and taking the steps to bring it into the world, there would be no book.

And the fact that it is now in physical form speaks to the art and persistence of my editor/publisher/mentor, Maureen Ryan Griffin, whose love of words and writing kept me going and inspired me along the way. Her years of working with books and her publishing knowledge, as well as her ability to explain this *foreign language* to me in ways I could understand, helped me immensely.

I owe the beauty of the creative, artistic cover to my illustrator, Ambrea Wright, a very talented young woman who understood my vision of the nine rooms. She blended it in her own way to create this beautiful design.

And I'm very thankful for all my friends and family who were cheerleaders in keeping me moving forward!

## About the Author

Valerie Althoff was born on a small farm outside of St. Paul, Minnesota. Since childhood she's been curious to know more about God, herself, and the world around her, and this has been the underlying theme of her life path.

Now that she is an elder herself, she has the desire to share some of the wisdom gained from all her life experiences. This book is her way of leaving a legacy for those who follow. And because every day brings new experiences and greater wisdom, there will be more to come.

Valerie welcomes invitations to speak and give classes to anyone who's interested in going deeper into awareness.

www.avisioninplace.com

Made in the USA
Columbia, SC
17 January 2020